The Porsche 911 and derivatives

The Porsche 911
and derivatives

A collector's guide
by Michael Cotton

MOTOR RACING PUBLICATIONS LTD
Unit 6, The Pilton Estate, 46 Pitlake, Croydon CR0 3RY, England

ISBN 0 947981 03 9
First published 1980
Reprinted 1980
Reprinted 1981
Reprinted 1983
Second Edition 1985
Reprinted 1987

Printed in Great Britain by Netherwood, Dalton & Co Ltd,
Bradley Mills, Huddersfield, West Yorkshire

Contents

technical art

Introduction

In the five years since the first edition of *Porsche 911 and Derivatives* was published, much has happened to prove that Professor Dr Ferry Porsche's company is a living, dynamic organization. The world's motor industry has been through a desperately depressing time shedding many thousands of workers in the effort to become more cost-effective, more competitive and more profitable. By contrast the family-owned sports car firm in the Zuffenhausen suburb of Stuttgart has increased its labour force from 5,000 to a little over 6,000. Turnover and profits have risen steadily year by year and the Weissach research and development centre, which celebrated its 50th anniversary in 1981, now employs a quarter of Porsche's workforce.

Production of the 911, 924, 944 and 928 models now exceeds 45,000 cars annually, and considerable effort and expense is being devoted to modernize the Zuffenhausen Works II (the industrial centre) in order to produce more 911 and 928 models.

A new chief executive, Peter W. Schutz, was appointed on the first day of 1981, and his first act was to extend the life of the greatly loved 911 model, at least through the 1980s and, who knows, maybe to the milestone year of 2 000. The 200,000th 911 was manufactured in September 1981, and the 250,000th is due to roll out in the early part of 1986.

A cabriolet model (long overdue), the Carrera version, and the exciting four-wheel-drive 959 derivative all made their debuts in the early 1980s, and much more is in the pipeline to maintain the evergreen appeal of this flat-six, rear-engined sports car that first appeared in September 1963, before many of our readers were born.

The company's structure has been modernized a little, too, with the flotation of shares on the Stock Exchange in 1984 whereby a third of the capital, amounting to 35 DM million, has been put into public hands. The 10 family shareholders, however, members of the Porsche and Piëch families, continue to hold the voting rights.

Also in 1984, on the occasion of his 75th birthday, Dr Porsche was conferred with the title of Professor by the Prime Minister of Baden-Württemberg, Herr Lothar Späth, who said in his presentation: 'Your exceptional creativity, your foresight and your initiative have been the foundation and driving force behind the success of the Porsche company.'

On the sporting front, four more outright successes at Le Mans have brought Porsche's tally to nine, equalling Ferrari's record, and within a few months the figure may well rise to 10. The racing car, powered basically by the 911's air-cooled alloy engine, won three World Championship for Makes crowns with consummate ease. The 911 model won the arduous Paris-Dakar Raid comfortably at its first attempt in January 1984, and another version of the same engine was granted its certificate of airworthiness. And Dipl Ing Hans Mezger, one of Professor Porsche's many geniuses at Weissach, headed the team that designed the TAG Turbo Formula 1 engine which, in its first full season, completely dominated the world of Grand Prix racing to put Niki Lauda and Alain Prost streets ahead of their rivals. There were many people who said that Porsche could only design good sports cars, but you don't hear that any more!

This book, though, is all about the Porsche 911 models and its derivatives, through from the 934 and 935 racing cars to the 959, which went into production in April 1985. The 935 has had its day now, after winning 42 World Championship races and some 70 IMSA events in the United States, surely one of the company's most successful competitions designs. It even won at Le Mans (in 1979), a unique achievement in modern times for a production-based machine. The 911 itself won the Monte Carlo Rally four times, and I feel that I now have more justification than ever in asserting that the Porsche 911 is the finest sports car the world has ever seen, even against the best that Bugatti, Ferrari, Jaguar, Bentley *et al* could offer. Compact, responsive, drivable and thoroughly enjoyable, the 911 has always been able to deliver more than the owner or spectator could reasonably expect for a car of its capacity. Its engine has been refined, enlarged, turbocharged, water-cooled in racing form and tuned to as much as 750 bhp, but the original design by Ing Hans Tomala, and its subsequent development by Dr Ferdinand Piëch, remains intact.

Demand for the 911 remains as strong as ever, more than 14,000 being produced in the 1984 model year, and provisions to scrap the design at this time have been shelved. The 911 is, and will remain, a true classic. Later designs and more modern concepts from Weissach have gained widespread acceptance, but can never surpass the particular appeal of the 911.

In addition to those I thanked in introducing the first edition, including John Dunbar and London Art Tech, Colin Taylor, Peter Tempest and Jerry Sloniger, I would now like to acknowledge the extra contributions of the Porsche Cars Great Britain Limited Press Office, Paul Davies, Klaus Parr, Juergen Barth and above all Klaus Reichert at the Porsche factory for providing the cover picture which captures the spirit of this book.

MICHAEL COTTON

February 1985

8

CHAPTER 1

Ancestors and parentage

From VW Beetle to type 356

Porsche like to think of themselves as the biggest of the small manufacturers, in a rôle that does not bring the Stuttgart-Zuffenhausen company into direct competition with higher volume quality car manufacturers such as Daimler-Benz or BMW. Yet the fact is that over the years, and especially in the last decade, Porsche's philosophy has matured considerably. The family-owned firm still makes sports cars, certainly, but they are luxurious and sophisticated, honed in competitions yet fully equipped to appeal to the wealthy and discriminating customer.

The Porsche story, inevitably, dates back to the birth of Ferdinand Porsche in 1875, in Maffersdorf, Bohemia. Showing an unusual creative genius, he installed electric lighting in the family home when he was 16 years of age (it was the first house to be so equipped for miles around) and at the age of 25 he had his first car displayed in the Paris exhibition. This was the electric hub-driven Lohner-Porsche, and the first car constructed was sold to a Mr E.W. Hart, in Luton. By the age of 30 he was technical director of the Austrian Daimler company and several very successful designs came during the following years, notably the Prince Henry Austro-Daimler of 1910. In 1924 he was appointed technical director of the Daimler company in Stuttgart, where he was responsible for such designs as the Mercedes-Benz 'S' and 'SSK' supercharged cars.

Six years later, via the Steyr concern in Austria, Dr Ferdinand Porsche, as he had become, decided to set up his own technical design studio in Stuttgart. His first commission was a six-cylinder passenger car for Wanderer, and a most exciting project soon followed — to design and build a Grand Prix car for Auto Union. This was the first successful rear-engined racing machine, with a supercharged V16 engine located behind the driver, who sat well forward in the chassis, and most of the early test work was carried out by his eldest son, Ferdinand 'Ferry' Porsche. While this advanced racing car (which had torsion-bar suspension) was duelling with the Mercedes-Benz Grand Prix car on the circuits of Europe, Porsche's new project was the design of the Volkswagen. After receiving the go-ahead from the German Government in 1934, Porsche had hand-built prototypes running in 1935 and the following year he was assigned to design and construct the Wolfsburg factory in which these cars were to be made. In fact the first production car was seen at the Berlin motor show in 1939, and although only a handful were made for customers before World War 2 began, several variants served the German forces during the next few years.

Porsche, officially discouraged from manufacturing a sports car version of the Volkswagen, did in fact build three superbly aerodynamic coupé versions with increased horsepower for an event planned for late-1939, the Berlin-to-Rome rally, which was intended to underline the relationship between the two Fascist regimes. The race did not take place, but the type 64 coupé has its place in history because it was certainly a forerunner of the 356 model on which the Porsche manufacturing dynasty was founded.

Professor Porsche was interned by the French after the war, and his son, Ferry, continued the family consultancy assisted by Erwin Kommenda. Their first postwar project was the design of the Cisitalia Formula 1 car for Carlo Dusio, the fee for this project paying the ransom for the Professor's release.

The 356 was finally assembled in June 1948, and at the time Ferry believed that there might be a market for 50 or so cars,

Where it all started — the Porsche family home in Feuerbacher Weg, Stuttgart, showing the garage in which the first Volkswagen prototype was built in 1935.

providing they could obtain the materials and all the correct permits to build and export the products.

'Number 1' was an alloy-bodied tubular-framed roadster built, in Austria, purely upon Volkswagen components, though the engine and transmission had been turned around to give it a mid-engined configuration. The old Professor, finally released from internment, approved the design, but suggested that the engine should be placed right at the back in order to provide a little space behind the seats, either for luggage or for small children.

The prototype had an 1,131-cc four-cylinder engine developing just 40 horsepower, and the complete car weighed 1,340 lb. At this stage Herr R. von Senger arrived from Zurich and immediately ordered five cars which he thought he could sell in Switzerland, though these would be a coupé design which he had not even set eyes upon. Kommenda restyled the 356 in its coupé form, the most significant design feature now being a platform chassis, and the engine was 'souped up' to 44 horsepower with the help of a higher compression and twin carburettors. At the same time the VW front axle was improved, the front brakes were converted from cable to hydraulic operation, and the front dampers were made bigger. The weight of the coupé was 1,550 lb, still with aluminium bodywork.

In the next two years a further 48 coupés were built laboriously by hand. The panel-beater was a master craftsman named Friedrich Weber, a genius no doubt, but one who had a tendency to slide away for liquid refreshment; but still, it took him two months to make the prototype, and the production rate settled down at around one car per fortnight, and gratifyingly they were almost invariably sold before they had been made. Perhaps the estimate of 50 cars had been much too low.

Despite the low power output, the Porsche 356, with a top speed of 90 mph, was the fastest car in production in Germany. Compared with the rather austere products generally offered for sale it was a breath of fresh air in the motor industry, and critics praised it highly for its good handling (which might seem rather strange nowadays, when the vices of swing-axles are best forgotten!), nimble performance, good fuel economy and general roadability. In fact Porsche knew something which most car manufacturers almost invariably failed to realise, namely that low weight was the solution to many problems. As Ferdinand Piëch, nephew of Dr Porsche and designer of Porsche's most successful racing designs in the late-'60s explained to me: 'The lighter you make the car, the less weight there is to brake for a corner, to take around the corner, and to accelerate from the corner.' So obvious, so simple! This dictum has always been pursued in all Porsche products and must be the clue to the success achieved by a great variety of road and track designs.

In 1949 a contract was drawn up with the Reutter company in Stuttgart to manufacture the body-chassis units, now in steel, and meanwhile a new cylinder-head with inclined, larger valves was designed for the VW flat-four engine. Production was transferred from Gmünd to Stuttgart, where Ferry Porsche rented space in a barracks, and in September 1949 the production of Porsche sports cars began seriously.

The 356 model merits a book in itself, but for now here are just a few facts and figures as a necessary preamble to the introduction of the 911. In 1950, the first full year of series production, 298 cars were produced. The following year, 1,182 cars were made and found an enthusiastic market. Noting that Professor Porsche died early in 1951, leaving the company in the hands of his son, Ferry, we move on to the year 1955, when no fewer than 2,952 Porsche 356A sports cars were made, by this time in the 'Works 1' factory which was now entirely Porsche's. By 1959, when the further improved 356B model was announced, annual production had risen to 7,055 units, and now the marque Porsche was securely established with a worldwide reputation.

When the 356 series was discontinued in 1965 a total of 76,305 cars had been built. Engine capacity had risen through 1,300 cc to 1500, and eventually 1,600 cc, and normal power output had risen to 95 horsepower. Four distinct versions had been produced, each one subtly better than its predecessor . . . yet the writing was on the wall. Since the late-'50s Porsche's designers had been working on a totally new model, designated the 901, which had a new yet distinctively Porsche-styled body shape. Most significantly, it was to be powered by an entirely new six-cylinder, 2-litre engine, and it would take over completely from the 356 series in 1965. What a gamble, to discontinue a model upon which the entire company was dependent and replace it with something which was, in today's parlance, very up-market! Yet the formula worked. With the four-cylinder 912 version augmenting production of the 911 (the type number was changed when Peugeot objected, having registered the zero middle digits themselves), production in 1966 was the highest ever at 13,134 cars. A new legend was born, and Porsche's future was secure.

This 'Type 7' prototype designed by Ferdinand 'Butzi' Porsche was the forerunner of the type 901 which appeared in the autumn of 1963. It was built by Reutter and has a wet-sump six-cylinder engine mounted at the rear.

Typical example of a Porsche 356, this being an 'A', which was manufactured from 1955 to 1959. In the 17 years from the first 356 in 1948 to the last in 1965 a total of around 76,000 were built.

CHAPTER 2

Birth of the 911

901 avoids a French connection

Clearly a company the size of Porsche could concentrate on no more than one model at a time, so the replacement for the 356 was the most important decision ever to face Dr Ferry Porsche and his assistants. From the outset Dr Porsche insisted that the wheelbase should not exceed 2.20 metres (86.6 inches), or 100 mm (3.9 inches) greater than that of the 356, so as to allow adequate space for 'plus-2' seating in the rear for children. If the car was to be used purely as a two-seater the extra space would be useful for luggage.

Dr Porsche's eldest son, Ferdinand 'Butzi', undertook the styling, and drawings of the 'type 7' date back to 1956. His brief was to design a shape which would be a recognizable successor to the 356, and from some angles — especially those involving the front and rear parts of the body — it did, and still does, remind one of the original car. Erwin Kommenda, the company's body engineer, was briefed to develop the design for production and four prototypes were made. One, which went beyond Dr Porsche's brief, was a full four-seater car, but this project was soon killed on the grounds that Porsche would not produce a family car in direct competition with Daimler-Benz, just a few kilometres removed in the city of Stuttgart. Interestingly, a very similar discussion developed when the 928 was under development in 1974 when, in the wake of the oil crisis, it was thought by many people that the era of sports cars was over. Then, as before, the argument prevailed that so long as cars are made there will always be a market for sports models which offer a special enjoyment of driving, and so a full four-seater version was dropped.

Finally scotching Kommenda's plans to enlarge the type 7 concept, Dr Porsche invited Reutter to develop a chassis for Butzi's design, within the parameters that it *would* be a 2-plus-2, but with enlarged luggage space, better handling and more comfort than the 356, with the performance of the 2-litre 356 Carrera, but with the refinement of the 1600-cc version. The type 7 would have no grease points, and maintenance was to be minimal. Faced with a *fait accompli* Kommenda quickly reconsidered the matter and set to with a will to develop the car that Dr Porsche had wanted all along.

In order to enlarge the luggage area, a very compact form of front suspension was designed. Longitudinal torsion-bars provided the springing medium, attached to a chassis cross-member at the rear and to a lower wishbone pivot at the front. Slim MacPherson struts housed telescopic dampers, but without the conventional coil springs. This allowed plenty of space for a roomy locker at the front, a low body line, and for 62 litres (13.6 gallons) of fuel to be carried in a flat, moulded tank forming the floor of the front locker. One idea, quickly abandoned on the recommendation of Reutters, was to have an opening rear window to facilitate luggage loading in the rear seat space.

Transverse torsion-bars were retained for the rear springing, but the most important design feature here was the abandoning of swing-axles in favour of semi-trailing arms, the triangular-link suspension now finding general favour in passenger-car development. Handling would be improved, and vice-free, and comfort would be better, too.

The heart of any car is the power plant, and here, too, something entirely new would be needed. The flat-four Carrera engine, designed by Dr Ernst Fuhrmann (later to become

Porsche's managing director), was originally intended to be a pure racing unit of 1,500 cc, with roller bearings and twin camshafts on each bank. Although 'productionized' in 2-litre form with plain bearings, it was altogether too expensive and too difficult to maintain for series manufacture.

Under the direction of Ing Hans Tomala, design proceeded on a full 2-litre, six-cylinder engine which would be overhung at the rear. Six cylinders would produce the required smoothness, and it was a case of Hobson's choice for the rear location. Dr Porsche firmly believed that in the light of all his experience of racing cars, the front-engined configuration would fall increasingly from favour in future years. Ideally, the engine should be in the mid-position, as with racing cars, but this would not allow enough space for occupants; he was convinced that an overhung engine, especially if it was constructed of light metals, would pose no particular problems, so design proceeded on that basis. Naturally, the unit would be air-cooled, and quite early on it was decided to

adopt a single overhead camshaft on each bank of cylinders. Toothed-belt drive was considered in the interests of quietness (just one company, Glas, was using such belts at the time), but this idea was shelved in favour of high-quality Reynolds chains with an hydraulic tensioner for each bank.

Oil-cooled cylinders were also considered in the interests of quietness, but did not meet expectations, and the definitive prototype of the type 901 engine was the experimental type 821, which was similar in most respects, but had a wet sump. The man who actually takes credit for the final design is Ferdinand Piëch, who became head of engine development in 1964, and chief of development two years later.

The type 901 was unveiled at the Frankfurt show in September 1963, though it was not scheduled for production until 12 months later. It created quite a sensation for, while the family likeness was maintained, it had greater interior space, 50 per cent more glass area (the windscreen was deeper, for a start), a lower waistline and

A publicity photograph taken in 1964 showing the 901 with the still contemporary 356 line-up. The 911, though longer and lower than the 356, was actually narrower with less rounded curves.

less bulbous styling, and it was actually 2.4 inches narrower than the 356, with less overhang outside the wheels. The wheelbase was five inches greater but the overall length was a mere six inches greater, thanks to the integrated bumper-bar structure. The car appeared altogether crisper and cleaner than the 356, and had a drag coefficient of 0.381 to prove it; whereas the 356 had started out with a drag coefficient of 0.375, it had risen to 0.40 with the introduction of higher bumpers on the 356B.

Design features included disc brakes on all four wheels, of ATE design, the rear discs incorporating small drums at the hubs for efficient handbrake operation. Rack-and-pinion steering was adopted, and the safety steering column incorporated two universal joints for improved safety.

The engine was fully air-cooled, as would be expected, with a vertical belt-driven fan enclosed in a plastic housing. Some of the air was diverted on to the exhaust system heat exchangers and thence, through flap valves controlled from the driving seat, to the interior for heating purposes.

The cast-aluminium crankcase was split vertically at the centreline of the forged steel crankshaft, which ran in eight bearings, and the six pistons ran in individual, heavily finned barrels with chromed bores. Dry-sump lubrication was specified, the tank being located in the right-hand rear panel. Bore and stroke dimensions were substantially 'over-square' at 80 × 66 mm, giving a capacity of 1,991 cc and plenty of scope for future increases. Through the years, capacity was increased

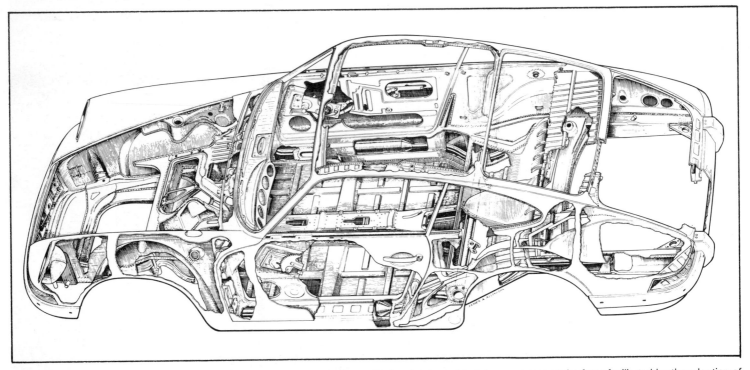

Chassis cutaway of the 911 indicating the full monocoque structure, with a wide luggage/petrol tank compartment at the front facilitated by the adoption of MacPherson struts and longitudinal torsion bars. At Dr Porsche's insistence the 911 was a two-plus-two-seater, and the final drag figure was 0.38.

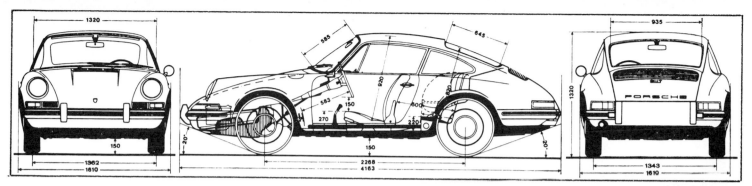

Vital statistics of the Porsche 911, which have changed very little over the years apart from the lengthening of the wheelbase in 1969.

Dashboard layout of the 911, circa 1964. A large-diameter wood-rim steering wheel has four spokes, and good sized bars for horn operation. With dry-sump lubrication, the instrumentation included an oil sump level gauge, still featured today. Note the rudimentary warm-air outlets below the doors.

progressively to 3.3 litres and, with turbocharging, the power rose to 300 horsepower. To start with, however, the power was restricted to 130 bhp DIN at 6,100 rpm, the torque curve peaking at 128 lb ft at 4,200 rpm. With three triple-choke Solex 40 P1 carburettors and a compression ratio of 9:1, the engine was predictably in a low state of tune with ample scope for development.

Drive was taken via a 215 mm-diameter Fichtel & Sachs single-plate clutch to an entirely new five-speed gearbox, naturally incorporating Porsche-patented synchromesh on all ratios. Second, third, fourth and fifth ratios were in the normal H-pattern, with first and reverse away to the left with a spring detente. Finally, drive was taken to the wheels by means of fully articulated drive-shafts, with Nadella joints inboard and Hooke

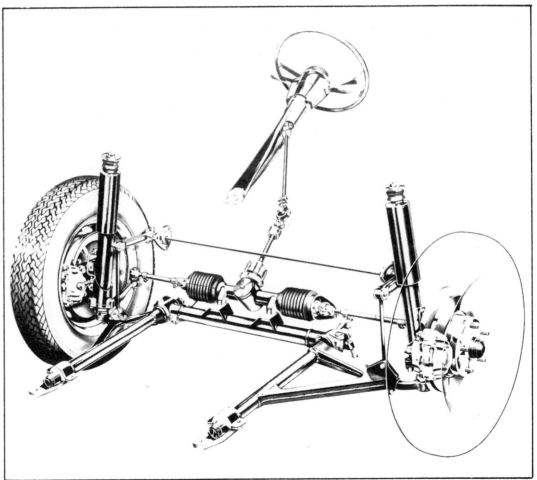

Front suspension and 'pot' steering layout of the early 911 (right-hand drive) showing the forward-running torsion bars, inclined dampers and universally jointed steering column.

joints outboard. Steel wheels of 15-inch diameter were fitted, with unusually narrow 165-section tyres mounted on 4½-inch wide rims. The philosophy was that narrow rims would be needed to accommodate the camber changes, but such ideas were fairly deeply rooted in the past.

As shown in 1963 the Porsche type 901 weighed 1,080 kg (2,380 lb, or a little over 21 cwt), the engine itself weighing 184 kg (406 lb) complete with clutch. Maximum speed of the car was 131 mph, and it would accelerate from rest to 60 mph in 8.5 seconds, and to 100 mph in 22.7 seconds.

The reception given to the 901 at Frankfurt was sufficiently encouraging for Dr Porsche to press on with the development of the Stuttgart-Zuffenhausen works in preparation for the newcomer, which had been scheduled for production in August 1964, initially alongside the 356C model. A stage in this development included taking over the nearby Reutter coachworks, which doubled the company's ground area.

The pricing structure was interesting, for the 901 was listed in Germany at 22,900 Deutschemarks, compared with 15,950 DM for the 'basic' 1,600-cc 356C and as much as 23,700 DM for the Carrera 2 Coupé, which was the nearest equivalent. It would not do, therefore, to phase-out the 356 until an equivalent model was derived from the 901 — or the 911 as it was officially redesignated before production began, following that official complaint from Peugeot. Even today, incidentally, many components are prefixed '901' in the parts list.

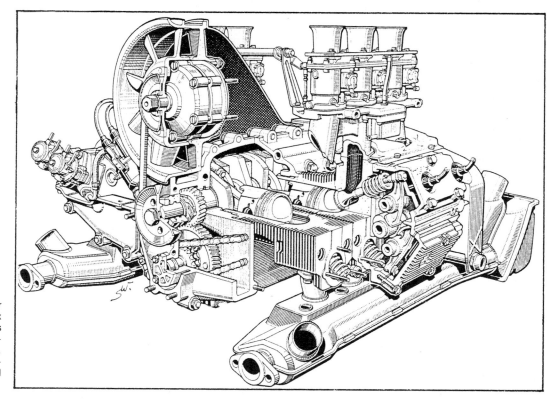

The original six-cylinder 'boxer' power unit, fitted with a triple-choke Solex carburettor on each bank. The unit has dry-sump lubrication, and the forged-steel crankshaft has eight main bearings. Following tradition, the engine is air-cooled for lightness, simplicity and reliability.

17

The 911's cast-alloy crankcase, a light but sturdy design with large bearing journals. The individual, finned cylinder barrels are bolted on to the case on either side during assembly.

The three individual heads on each bank of cylinders are bridged by an alloy cam box casting enclosing the camshaft and rockers.

Schematic view of the original 901/0 five-speed gearbox, inboard of the rear-mounted power unit.

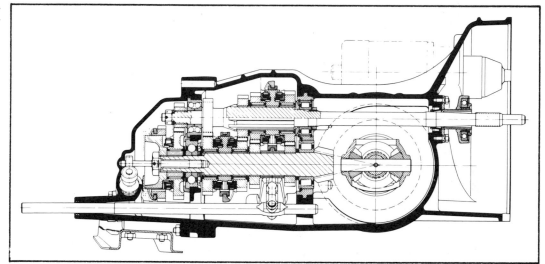

Rear suspension layout, left, showing the innovative semi-trailing-arm design in conjunction with transverse torsion bars. Note too the parking brake within the disc, right, a familiar Porsche feature.

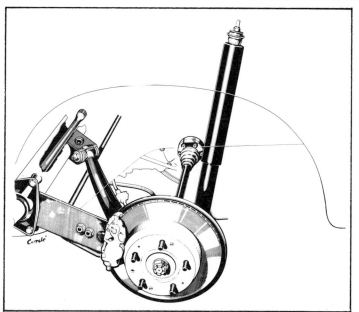

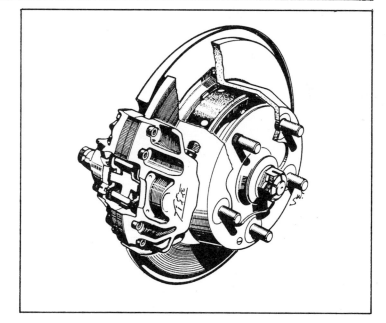

CHAPTER 3

'Everyman's Porsche'

912 fills a gap

There was certainly a need for a less expensive model to plug the gap between the old and new generations, and it would necessarily be a four-cylinder-engined version to serve this purpose. The 912 version of the 911 retained most of the new mechanical elements, but substituted the 356C's pushrod, four-cylinder engine of 1,600-cc, coupled to a four-speed gearbox (as standard) or the new five-speed transmission, which cost an extra 340 DM.

The 1,600-cc unit was, in fact, slightly detuned from 95 to 90 horsepower in the quest for greater smoothness and flexibility, and an air-intake silencer accounted for some power, too. Two twin-choke carburettors were employed, and the red line on the tachometer was raised from 5,500 to 6,000 rpm; improved torque was also claimed. Another alteration was the adoption of 12-volt ignition, in place of the 6-volt system employed previously.

Obviously the main appeal of the 912 over the earlier car was the smarter body shape and the improved accommodation. The doors were bigger, the glazed area substantially increased, the seats were more comfortable, the luggage space was greater, and so on. As on the 911, an improved instrument console was provided with three large, clear instruments directly in front of the driver. The dashboard was padded on the upper and lower edges, and incorporated a larger glove locker.

Even with all these improvements the 912 was not a model which particularly appealed to Porsche enthusiasts, even though the price announced in April 1965 was just 16,250 DM. Despite its lower weight compared with the 911 model (970 kg) the top speed of 115 mph and 0-60 mph acceleration time of around 12 seconds would not have been described as scintillating, and there

were some pretty hot production family cars like the Lotus-Cortina coming along that could out-perform the 912 at much lower cost.

Yet, no doubt *because* it was a Porsche, the 912 would be deemed a successful model. To start off it was only offered on the continent of Europe because, even then, there were various type-approval problems for America. Even so 6,440 cars were made in the first year, alongside 4,865 911 models, and production rose to 8,700 units the following year when the American market was opened up.

Sales appeal improved in September 1965 (some five months after the model's announcement) when Targa versions of this and the 911 were announced. Three years later there were some revisions, in common with the 911, notably increasing the wheelbase by 57 mm (2.24 inches) to 2,268 mm (89.3 inches) in the quest for better handling. At the same time the track was increased marginally with the introduction of thicker brake discs, wheelarches were slightly flared, the steering wheel diameter was reduced, and there were a number of cosmetic changes to the interior. Light-alloy rims were obtainable to special order, either 5.5 × 14-inch or 6 × 15-inch.

The 912 is unusual in motoring history, if not unique, in having ceased production only to be reintroduced six years later. A production total of 30,300 by the end of 1968 was entirely satisfactory, but the model was dropped to make way for the mid-engined 914/4 and 914/6 models to be produced at the Karmann factory by the new joint stock company, VW-Porsche. As is now history, the six-cylinder Porsche-powered two seater model lasted little more than two years, being priced too close to the 911 to

Effectively replacing the 356 model, the 912 retained the four-cylinder 90 bhp power unit within the new body shell. It was less lavishly equipped and was listed at DM 16,250 with four-speed transmission, or DM 340 extra with five speeds. A Targa version became available later on.

have any real sales impact, but the four-cylinder Volkswagen-powered 'base model' continued through to 1975, predominantly by being successful in America. In all some 115,000 914s were made, of which 89,000 were shipped to the United States.

When the VW-Porsche's life came to an end the 912 was reintroduced as a stop-gap model, at the insistence of the Porsche-Audi marketing organization in the States, until the new Porsche 924 design came along. In its new form the 912 was designated the 912E, with the 1,971-cc Volkswagen four-cylinder engine equipped with Bosch L-Jetronic fuel injection. It was, in fact, virtually identical to the power unit from the 914/4 which, with emission equipment installed, developed 90 bhp at 4,900 rpm. The level of equipment was slightly reduced compared with the then current 911 model, and in total 2,099 cars were produced in a year, solely for the American market.

The Porsche 924 was announced towards the end of 1975, effectively superseding the 912E. This, too, had a VW-Audi-based engine of 2-litres, but producing 125 bhp in European form, and 110 bhp for the States, and the model could be said to have entered the market where the 911 had been launched 11 years previously. By this time the 911 had been enlarged to 2.7 litres, soon rising to a full 3 litres (in SC form), and whereas production of the 911 model at Zuffenhausen was steady at *circa* 15,000 units per annum, the 924 was to be built at the Audi plant in Neckarsulm at a rate of 24,000 units per annum — quite an advance.

Reintroduced as a 912E after a gap of six years, the four-cylinder Porsche is seen here in Targa form in the company of 911S and Carrera Coupés.

CHAPTER 4

Improving the breed

O-series, A-series and B-series models

It is always easy, with hindsight, to see the deficiencies of previous car models. Were this not so, progress would not be made. Whenever a 'traditional' manufacturer like Porsche brings out something new there will be people who doubt if things will ever be the same again, and certainly many customers lamented the passing of the 356 — probably Dr Porsche and his employees did, too. Yet if Porsche lost any customers, which is doubtful, they found a whole lot more, for in 1966, the first year of full production of the 912 and 911 models combined, sales hit a new peak of 13,134 cars. Some of the bodies were being made by the Karmann works to ease the production difficulties, and the total labour force was now approaching the 4,000 mark.

From the beginning, the 911 has been a scintillating car to drive. It is not a compromise between the stylist, the engineer and the accountant, as so many mundane models tend to be, but a taut, willing package designed and built by people who care most about driving pleasure. The engine response is crisp, the harsh note thrilling, the brakes extremely reassuring, and the handling positive . . . well, in the early days they were working on it!

From the outset the main concern was oversteer resulting from the positioning of the engine, and the narrow rims and tyres merely contributed to the rather sudden breakaway which could be achieved when the limits were explored. By today's standards the handling of the early models would be reckoned poor, but in 1964 it was acceptable with the reservation that the car needed to be treated with a little respect. Also of concern to the development team was the tendency for the 911 to *understeer* pretty badly at normal speeds, due to the light loading at the front, and the need to adjust the front and rear suspension geometries accordingly. It was many years before Paul Frère was able to reveal the truth, that if a customer complained loudly enough his 911 would be secretly 'doctored' with the installation of 11 kg lead weights behind each end of the front bumpers which, being flush-fitted, did not reveal their presence. Ing Tomala left the Porsche company in 1966 to be succeeded as head of development by Ferdinand Piëch, who applied more scientific approaches to the solution. During the next five years the adoption of wider rims and tyres and different geometries, and eventually the lengthening of the wheelbase to alter the weight distribution, brought about great improvements, while the following five years saw tremendous advances in aerodynamics, with the development of air dams and rear wings, which completed the transformation.

The world's motoring Press was invited to drive the first production cars in the autumn of 1964, and their praise was unanimous. *Car and Driver* recorded a standstill-to-60 mph acceleration figure of 7.0 seconds with a maximum speed of 130 mph, results which proved that the new model was indeed quicker than the 356 Carrera. In particular, the performance of the engine impressed everybody with its smooth, vivid acceleration to the limit of 6,800 rpm. Some found it rather tiring to maintain high speeds on account of engine and wind noise, one or two commented on the rather direct steering, and most complained about a carburation flat-spot between 2,500 and 3,200 rpm; although Solex had developed a floatless carburettor especially for this model, it was not without its problems, and the majority of customers were to complain in due course.

Porsche were swamped with orders, and the real problem arose

The original Targa model had a folding rear window panel, though later on a fixed-position glass rear screen was standardized. The Targa option was introduced with the A-series cars in August 1967 and was an immediate success.

of satisfying the demand. The recently acquired Reutter company, which had virtually doubled the size of the company, was unable to cope, so the Karmann works was given an order to put 911/912 bodies into production as well, with final assembly taking place at Zuffenhausen.

The loss of an open-top car was a break with Porsche's tradition, and the gap in the range was filled with the announcement of the Targa top at the Frankfurt show in September 1965, with availability the following year. Provided for both the 911 and the 912, the Targa consisted of a substantial safety roll-over hoop, finished in satin-look stainless steel, with a lift-out roof section in two forms — either a rigid plastic section, or a collapsible framed hood which could be stowed away in the front locker. Behind the roll-over hoop was a zip-out rear section containing a plastic rear window.

The logic of this was sound, for as car speeds increased the problems associated with convertibles became ever more difficult to solve, the main ones being buffetting and noise. A true convertible can be very tiring to drive at speed for hours at a time, due mainly to the rush of air which is swept *forwards*, and the possibility of leaving the rear window in place solved this at a stroke. Certainly, in a country where *autobahn* travel is popular, the new Porsche Targa became a winner straight away, and the production rate of seven Targas per day (out of a total production of 55 cars) was soon found to be totally inadequate. In the next 12 months Targa production was pushed up to as much as 40 per cent of the total production.

At an early stage in the 911's life it was realised that the car was slightly over-geared, perhaps due to needless worries about reliability, and in July 1965 the six-cylinder model was given the set of lower gearbox ratios (type 902) developed for the four-cylinder 912 model. The gap between second and third was reduced, and although improvements in acceleration times were insignificant it gave the 911 better pickup in the gears, while maximum speed was attained at 6,700 rpm instead of 6,400 rpm.

Competition involvement forms an integral part of Porsche's development, and continues to do so at the present time. Unlike other manufacturers who enter racing or rallying then bow out, perhaps in a blaze of glory, a few years later, Porsche almost spurns the publicity aspect, but makes very good use of the technical feedback. Indeed, the same engineers who attend the world's race tracks return to Weissach on Monday to carry on developing a new camshaft, clutch plate or whatever for next year's road car. The 911 made its competitions debut on the Monte Carlo Rally in January 1965, when Porsche's development engineers Herbert Linge and Peter Falk finished in fifth place overall, and meanwhile a similar six-cylinder engine was being prepared for the Targa Florio in May.

This unit, equipped with Weber carburettors, was constructed largely of magnesium alloy in order to reduce weight, and had titanium con-rods and twin ignition. Otherwise it was production-based, and developed 210 bhp at 8,000 rpm. Fitted into a 904 racing car, this engine proved completely reliable and rather more flexible than the racing eight-cylinder unit, and it took Herbert Linge and Umberto Maglioli into second place.

By February 1966 the factory had given up completely with the Solex carburation system and had adopted, instead, Weber IDA 30 3C carburettors, which completely cured the flat-spot problem; at this time the engine was redesignated the 901/05 unit. Twin mechanical fuel pumps were now unnecessary as the Webers had normal float chambers, and the engine was correspondingly more flexible than hitherto.

A car that enthusiastic drivers had been waiting for was announced in July 1966 for the 1967 model year — the 911S, with 160 horsepower. The type 911/02 unit installed differed in having new camshafts with considerably more overlap, larger valves and improved porting, forged rather than cast pistons with

The 100,000th Porsche produced was a 911 Targa equipped for the German police, and handed over on December 21, 1966. These 130 mph sports cars were easily capable of catching wrong-doers on the German *autobahn* system.

higher crowns raising the compression ratio from 9 to 9.8:1, and Weber type 40 IDS carburettors. Modifying the heat exchanger alone was said to account for an extra 10 horsepower, while an increase of 6 psi in recommended tyre pressures was also said to increase the maximum speed. Putting the finishing touches on the engine, the air duct shrouding was made of red plastic instead of black, and the most powerful engine in Porsche's production range has been identified this way ever since. Harder Bosch sparking plugs were fitted, and the maximum power output of 160 bhp was achieved at 6,600 rpm, while the maximum permitted engine speed rose to 7,300 rpm.

Visually, the 911S could be picked out immediately by the new forged-alloy, 'five spoke' polished wheels, which virtually became a Porsche trademark in years to come. These were far more

Originally the A.F.N. Limited demonstrator, MMU 911C was the first right-hand-drive 911 manufactured. Built in 1965, it has been renovated by a Midlands enthusiast, and now features the later alloy wheels.

The introduction of the 160 horsepower 911S in August 1966 gave the series extra appeal. 5½J forged-alloy rims with a spoke appearance became a Porsche hallmark, and masked the new internally ventilated disc brakes front and rear.

expensive than the traditional steel wheels, but they were five pounds lighter and they allowed more air to circulate around the brake discs, which were now internally ventilated and therefore thicker. The wheels, supplied by Fuchs, had 5J rims which, although an advance on the 4½J steel rims, were still conservative by contemporary standards. An anti-roll bar was now fitted at the rear as well as the front, and Koni dampers were specified for the first time.

The maximum speed of the 911S went up to 140 mph, and although the quoted 0-60 mph acceleration time of 7.4 seconds was still rather slower than *Road & Track's* time for the original 911, it was nevertheless very impressive, and could probably be bettered. Outstanding, too, was the 0-100 mph time of 20 seconds

achieved by *Autocar,* very little slower than the 18 seconds-to-100 mph time achieved by the Jaguar E-type with almost double the engine size. Driver comfort was not overlooked in the 911S either, for the steering wheel was now leather-covered, the car had proper carpets instead of rubber mats, and the dashboard was trimmed with leatherette. Already a successful model, the S version made the 911 a real enthusiast's car.

On the other side of the coin, the 911S now had a reputation for fouling its plugs in traffic, and bursts of acceleration were needed to make it run properly. On derestricted roads, though, it was a joy to drive, so responsive that overtaking ceased to be any problem, even on short stretches of straight highway. *Autocar* commented that above 3,000 rpm it was like another pair of

The power unit of the 911S, with 160 bhp at 6,600 rpm on tap. The main changes included soft-nitrided connecting-rods, forged pistons, modified cylinder-heads, larger valves and different timing.

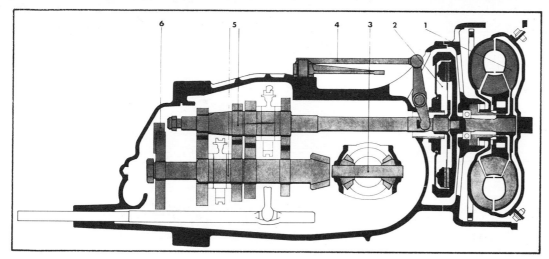

Sportomatic semi-automatic transmission, with four forward ratios, became available for the six-cylinder range from August 1967. To prove the two-pedal transmission two out of three cars entered for the Marathon de la Route — 84 hours around the Nurburgring — were so equipped, and provided the outright winner. Diagrammatic layout: 1 — hydraulic torque converter; 2 — clutch; 3 — differential; 4 — clutch linkage; 5 — 4-speed transmission; 6 — parking lock device.

The rack-and-pinion steering for the 1969-model B-series cars replaced the earlier 'pot' steering box with a more simple arrangement, which was designed for the 914 and was found to be cheaper to manufacture for the 911 series. Diagrammatic layout: 1 — thread for track rod ball-joint; 2 — housing; 3 — plunger; 4 — pressure spring; 5 — pinion; 6 — rack; 7 — dust cover; 8 — bearing bush.

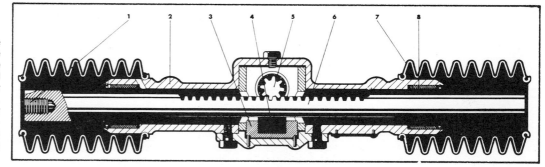

cylinders being switched on, and it was even possible to get wheelspin in top on wet roads.

The two-model line-up in the six-cylinder range became three in August 1967 when Porsche introduced the A-series, replacing the original O-series, and announced the 911T model (T was for Touring), rated at 110 horsepower. The 'normal' 911 became the 911L for the British market, and the S version was virtually unchanged.

It had been felt for some time that there was room for a lower-priced version, and the 911T was the first six-cylinder model to be offered at below 20,000 marks on the German market. With less power available, the finned alloy Biral cylinders in the 901/03 unit were replaced by cast-iron cylinders, and a cheaper crankshaft lacking counterweights was fitted. Steel rockers were replaced by similar components made of cast-iron, and these were successful enough to be fitted across the range the following year. The compression ratio was lowered to 8.6:1 and milder camshafts were fitted, although the expensive Weber carburettors were retained.

Interior equipment was similar to that of the 912, including solid brake discs, steel wheels, a four-speed gearbox and a lighter front anti-roll bar. The range now incorporated several

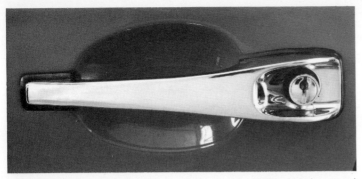

Visual changes on the A-programme starting in July 1967 included recessed door catch-push buttons and a larger exterior rear-view mirror. At the same time wheel-rim widths went up to 5½ inches, and the brakes had dual-circuit hydraulics.

improvements, notably 5½J wheel rim widths, recessed exterior door handles with push-button catches, quartz halogen fog lights, front seat-belt anchorage points, and matt black windscreen wiper arms which parked in front of the driver. In response to American legislation, which was beginning to affect car design, a dual hydraulic braking system was adopted, with separate front and rear circuits.

Additionally, 20 special cars with an R (for Racing) suffix were built during 1967 and proved extremely successful, but we'll come to those in another chapter.

For a long time Porsche had been toying with the idea of an automatic transmission for the American market, though with a degree of apprehension, and in 1967 they came up with the Sportomatic two-pedal transmission. This, it was felt, would meet the requirement for clutchless shifting but, with a normal gear lever and four forward speeds, would in no way destroy the 911's obviously sporting characteristics.

An electrical switch concealed in the gear lever knob actuated a solenoid connected to a vacuum reservoir, thus automatically disengaging the clutch merely at a touch of the gear lever. If nothing else, this cured drivers of bad habits if they were prone to holding on to the lever while driving along! This type 905 transmission, designed by Fichtel and Sachs, consisted of a three-element hydraulic torque converter, a single-plate diaphragm spring clutch and a normal four-speed gearbox, though with higher overall gearing (7/27 instead of 7/31).

This type of transmission was offered for 990 marks, and to give it good public acceptance Porsche entered two of their three cars with Sportomatic in the 84-hour Marathon de la Route, the former road rally now having been transferred to the Nurburgring. The five-speed 911S crashed during the event, and the 911S Sportomatic retired with a broken valve spring, but the Sportomatic-equipped 911R took a convincing victory in the hands of Hans Herrmann/Vic Elford/Jochen Neerpasch, thus overcoming any doubts the customers might have entertained about the transmission.

Performance, in fact, was hardly affected at all, adding perhaps a couple of tenths to the 60 mph acceleration time and shaving 3 mph off the top speed, while economy was, if anything, slightly improved. The torque converter made traffic driving a good deal more relaxing, and apart from that it cushioned the gear-changes

The most important single change in the 911's specification through the years was lengthening the wheelbase for the B-programme in August 1968. The rear wheels were moved back by 57 mm (2.24 in), extending the wheelbase to 2,268 mm, and the wheelarch was redesigned. As a quick indicator, the torsion bar adjustment covers were now partly concealed by the side rubbing strip. With 6-inch wheel rims now standardized, the front and rear arches are slightly flared.

sufficiently to mask all but the most clumsy shifts. Inevitably the reception to Sportomatic was rather sceptical, but it became popular among city drivers. In 1975, with the advent of 3-litre production engines, the Sportomatic was redesigned and given three forward speeds, all that was judged necessary considering the greatly improved torque. But with a less suitable selection of ratios on offer the performance was then noticably impaired, and oddly enough it was the American market which rejected Sportomatic first. The Sportomatic transmission was finally laid to rest in May 1979.

The A-series 911s lasted but a year, being replaced in August 1968 by the B-series, which incorporated a great many changes. Perhaps the most important of these was increasing the wheelbase by 57 mm to 2,268 mm (2.24 inches, up to 89.3 inches) without altering the position of the engine. The wheelarches were moved back as well, making it difficult to see the change outwardly, and as intended the result was to reduce the overhang of the engine, thus beneficially altering the car's weight distribution.

To do this the semi-trailing arms were increased in length and the Nadella drive-shafts were replaced by new Löbro shafts incorporating Rzeppa constant-velocity joints, and these were tested at maximum speed over 20,000 kilometres before being put into production. In conjunction with this important change, the engine crankcase was lightened by 10 kg with the adoption of magnesium in place of aluminium (the transmission housing was similarly changed in specification within a few months), twin batteries were fitted at the front, and the weight distribution was altered from 41.5/58.5 to 43/57 per cent. At the same time wheel rim width was increased to six inches on the 911S, so that the sporting customers could enjoy the better handling to the full.

Another important innovation was the availability of Bosch mechanical petrol injection, which raised the 911S' power output from 160 to 170 horsepower. The 911E (E for Einspritzung, or injection), replacing the 911L, went up from 130 to 140 horsepower, and at the same time both engines were fitted with electronic ignition systems.

Numerous chassis changes were introduced for the B-series, which was possibly the most significant model change in the 911's history. Self-levelling hydro-pneumatic front struts were fitted to the 911E, and were available optionally for the 911S and

One of the most significant features of the B-programme for 1969 was the adoption of Bosch mechanical fuel-injection for the 911E and 911S, thereby raising their power outputs by some 10 bhp.

911T. The steering rack was simplified, and given a slightly lower ratio to dampen-out road shocks, but at the same time a smaller leather-covered steering wheel became standard on the more powerful versions. Larger front brake calipers were fitted, those on the 911S having aluminium front calipers with a greater swept area. Thicker ventilated discs were fitted on both the 911E and the 911S, increasing the track by 0.4 inch, and the suspension wishbones were now made in one piece; to accommodate the widened track, the wheelarches were slightly flared.

Comfort was improved, too. The self-levelling hydro-pneumatic struts, which dispensed with the normal torsion-bars, were introduced primarily to improve the ride, though they were somewhat controversial so far as handling was concerned, hence the optional availability for the 911S. The heating-and-ventilation system was greatly improved, with a three-speed fan blower being installed for the first time, though facia fresh-air vents were not to be introduced for some years.

The Targa version underwent a significant 'phase 2' operation with a wrap-round glass rear window replacing the plastic zip-up panel (which had never been the easiest of contraptions to operate and had not proved to be entirely waterproof). Air exit slots were let into the rollover hoop to improve the circulation of air inside the car, though the British market was not even to receive Targa tops until 1973!

Other changes for the B-series cars included an electrically heated rear window, quartz halogen main lights, hazard warning lights, and a more powerful 770-Watt generator in conjunction with twin 35 amp/hr batteries, one mounted each side of the front wheelarches. The fuse box was moved from the interior to the front locker compartment, a hand throttle was fitted between the seats, larger door pockets were installed, with the door opening trigger recessed into the armrest, a dipping mirror was fitted, and there were numerous other trim changes. Seen for the first time was a new instrument combining the oil pressure and level indicator, and to complete the picture deep pile carpets replaced the loop weave pattern.

The result of all these changes was quite dramatic for, with all the handling improvements coming into force, the 911 was a far more forgiving car to drive. No longer did it understeer markedly in the slow turns, and no longer did the tail snap out of line on the faster curves — looking back, one would say that Porsche had 'got it right at last'. The longer wheelbase played the most important part in this transformation, but the steering and suspension changes, the new battery location, the wider track and the lower-profile (70 per cent aspect ratio) tyres all played their part.

Acceleration and top speed of the 911E and 911S were better (the maximum was up to 143 mph for the S), braking was more progressive and reliable, and importantly the engine changes had virtually eliminated the dreadful proneness to foul the plugs in heavy traffic. Two more modifications not previously mentioned for the 911S were the addition of an extra oil-cooler, mounted in the front right wheelarch and fed with cold air from the front valance, and the adoption of an aluminium engine cover in place of the steel cover. Inevitably this programme of improvements had its price, and now the cheapest six-cylinder car, the 911T, cost 19,960 DM, the 911E 24,700 DM and the 911S close to 27,000 DM, edging the cars up into the luxury class.

One of the major differences between German manufacturers, such as VW and Porsche, and their counterparts in Britain, such as Leyland, is the level of on-going development. Changes take place not only annually, but almost monthly on the German production lines, and certainly at Porsche the engineers are not locked in constant battle with the accountants. Having got the 911's handling right, the engineers now felt that the car could use still more power. . . .

The 911T was introduced in 1967 with a 110 bhp version of the six-cylinder engine, and with a less expensive interior similar to that of the 912. Note the rubber floor mats. Being a lighter car, it was the obvious basis for competition models.

CHAPTER 5

Boring and stroking

2.2-litre and 2.4-litre models

With around 60 per cent of their production going to America, Porsche naturally had to pay close attention to the increasing amount of legislation coming into force across the Atlantic. The most pressing problem was the need to meet future exhaust-emission regulations which have become ever more stringent during the 1970s. Like other manufacturers, Porsche decided to increase the engine capacity, to endow their American-specification cars with better flexibility and similar, if not more performance. As a bonus, the European cars would simply be more powerful!

The first stage in this programme was the introduction of 2.2-litre engines in September 1969, by the simple expedient of increasing the bore from 80 to 84 mm while leaving the stroke at 66 mm. The B-series cars had now become the C-series, with other refinements, and for the European market the power figures showed very useful gains: the 911T (now on Zenith carburettors rather than Webers) was up from 110 to 125 horsepower, the 911E from 140 to 155 horsepower, and the 911S from 170 to 180 horsepower.

Possibly the gains in torque were even more significant, rising from 116 to 130 lb ft for the 911T at the same engine speed (4,200 rpm), from 130 to 141 lb ft for the 911E and from 134 to 147 lb ft for the 911S. It had always been said of the Porsches that they were fine on long, straight roads, but they needed to be 'rowed along with the gear lever' in hilly country. At this point Porsche set about changing the legend.

Together with the power increase came a larger-diameter Fichtel & Sachs clutch, up from 215 to 225 mm, with a sealed diaphragm-operated spring to give a lighter pedal pressure.

The most significant improvement to the chassis was in the area of the front suspension, where the upper anchorage points of the struts were moved forwards by 14 mm (0.55 inch) to reduce the front wheel trail. The effect of this was to make the steering lighter, and to reduce the feedback from the road to the steering wheel. Hydro-pneumatic front struts which dispensed with the torsion-bars became standard — for the time being — on the 911E, which was regarded as the 'soft' comfort model, and optional on the 911T. However, although these worked very well as self-levelling units, and would have been highly regarded in a family car, they did not appeal to Porsche customers and were phased out of production during the 1971 model year. On the other models, the abutment screws for the torsion-bars were modified for easier adjustment to the ride height.

Ventilated disc brakes were adopted at this point for the 911T, though with iron calipers, while the 911E and the 911S were now given light-alloy calipers. The 'T' was equipped with Zenith triple-choke carburettors instead of the more expensive Webers, and it benefitted from larger valves (46 mm inlet, 40 mm exhaust) so that all three models now had an identical cylinder-head design. Noteworthy, too, was the insertion of the plug thread direct into the aluminium face, instead of using a Helicoil insert.

Gearboxes underwent some changes for the 1970 model year, notably with the adoption of magnesium for the main casing, which further reduced the rear-end weight bias. The standard four-speed gearbox for the 911T was designated 911/00, while the uprated five-speed box for the 911E and 911S was designated 911/01, having been redesigned to cope with the higher torque rating of the 2.2-litre engines. ZF limited-slip differentials were available for all three versions, with the choice of 40 or 80 per cent slip factors.

Further efforts to reduce weight at the back included the use of aluminium for the engine bay covers and centre bumper sections on the 'E' and 'S', but perhaps the most relevant factor of all for anyone purchasing a used car today is the fact that the chassis was given a coating of Tectyl oil-based anti-corrosion treatment, which went a long way towards beating the corrosion menace. Looking back, you could say that the B-series marked the beginning of the 'long-life' era, which would improve the value of cars in their later life.

At the same time, the facia layout was improved, notably in that the indicator and wiper levers were repositioned so that they could be operated by the driver without need for him to move his hands from the steering wheel. A 'pause' wipe phase was introduced, the instruments were now installed in the facia with O-rings so that they could be removed easily, and the rear window demister now had a two-level intensity for clearing mist or ice. A rear window wiper became a popular option.

Targa models were now accounting for 26 per cent of the production, and the switch to lighter collapsible roof sections, which stowed away more conveniently in the front compartment, completed the transformation to a really all-weather car which could be converted from open to closed form in about two minutes (perhaps less with practice), which meant that the occupants stood much less risk of a soaking of it rained suddenly.

Production rose to 15,275 cars in 1969, although the four-cylinder model-mix fell from 44 per cent the previous year to a

In the late-1960s Porsche began to develop a new research and development centre at Weissach, some 20 kilometres away from the factory in Stuttgart. Now one of the most comprehensive of any in Europe, and deriving approximately half its revenue from outside contracts, the centre covers nearly half a million square metres and employs 1,600 people. It has its own variable-layout road circuit, steering pad, cross-country course and tank-testing ground.

A new dashboard layout was designed for the C-programme (this is a 911S). The ventilation system was a through-flow type (fresh air), and the separately adjustable heating and ventilation systems included a three-speed fan. Instruments were now secured by O-rings for easy installation and withdrawal.

mere 16 per cent as production tailed off, so clearly Porsche's profit margins were rising. Turnover rose from 330 DM million to 360 DM million, while the number of employees had risen to 3,713. Further expansion was in progress, and with up to 25 bodies per day still arriving from the Karmann works, the factory was capable of producing 80 cars every working day.

Following two years of intensive development under the direction of Ferdinand Piëch, which coincided with one of the most exciting periods in the firm's racing history as the 908 and 917 models were developed, no notable changes were seen on the 911 series from the autumn of 1969 until the autumn of 1971.

There were some minor technical changes, mainly to meet the emission laws creeping into some European countries, and these primarily concerned the ignition and fuel-injection systems. The

only visual change for the 1971 model, albeit hidden away, was the removal of the electric fuel pump from the front suspension cross-member to the rear of the car, between the main cross-member and the left-hand semi-trailing arm.

If 1970 was a year of consolidation, it was also the most successful year the Porsche company had yet had. No fewer than 16,761 cars were produced at the Zuffenhausen works, a total not to be exceeded throughout the rest of the decade. Annual turnover rose to a record 420 DM million. The year was also significant for the production of the 150,000th Porsche, a 911S which was ceremoniously handed over to David Nurse, a founder member of the Porsche Club of America.

The shareholders, all members of the Porsche and Piëch families, agreed to raise the share capital from 3 DM million to 20

The second major development in the 911's history was the start of the process of increasing engine capacity. The C-programme models starting in September 1969 had a 2.2-litre capacity, the bore increasing from 80 to 84 mm. Magnesium alloy replaced aluminium as the crankcase material, and the E and S versions had engine covers made of aluminium.

DM million to pay for the continuing rapid development of the factory. In September 1970 a completely new paint shop was opened at Schwieberdinger Strasse, creating 450 new jobs and introducing the electrophorese paint process which guaranteed an extremely good finish. After galvanizing and undercoating, four good coats of paint were applied to each body, sometimes with metallic tints, and a much wider range of colours could be introduced.

In fact, Porsche claimed to be able to offer cars in any colour the customer wished (at a price!). One lady customer is said to have sent a sample of her nail varnish, another a piece of material which matched the colour of her eyes, and these colours were indeed supplied. Sometimes the results were somewhat garish, but all the customers were happy, and that was what mattered.

One advantage of going over 2-litres was the possibility of running in the 2.5-litre class in racing, a subject that is always uppermost in the minds of everyone at Porsche. Nominally the engines were rated at 2,195 cc from the autumn of 1969, but the customers soon got busy increasing the bore from 84 to 85 mm, and later on to 87.5 mm, for plenty of room had been left in the

original design for cylinder enlargement. At 87.5 mm the Biral cylinder liners reached their limit of diameter, but while this was fine for competitions purposes (especially with twin-plug heads) it left little room for combustion in a production unit.

So instead, the factory decided to increase the capacity in the new E-series cars by increasing the stroke, and at the same time they effectively detuned the engine to enable it to meet America's increasingly stringent emission laws. Thus compression ratios were lowered, from 8.6 to 7.5:1 in the case of the 'T', from 9.1 to 8:1 in the 'E' and from 9.8 to 8.5:1 in the 'S' so that all three would run on regular-grade 91-octane (2-star, as we know it) fuel, although petrol pump attendants were normally disbelieving.

Power increased a little at the same time, though principally the engines became even more flexible, as the accompanying table shows:

	Bore (mm)	Stroke (mm)	Capacity (cc)	Power (bhp/rpm)	Torque (lb ft/rpm)	Compression ratio
911T, 1969-1971	84	66	2195	125/5800	130/4200	8.6
911E, 1969-1971	84	66	2195	155/6200	141/4500	9.1
911S, 1969-1971	84	66	2195	180/6500	147/5200	9.8
911T, 1971-1973	84	70.4	2341	130/5600	145/4000	7.5
911E, 1971-1973	84	70.4	2341	165/6200	152/4500	8.0
911S, 1971-1973	84	70.4	2341	190/6500	160/5200	8.5

The German police continued to be good customers of Porsche, usually favouring the Targa versions.

The internals of the engine were modified to some extent, for in conjunction with the longer-throw crankshaft the crankcase itself was given additional webbing for extra strength, the main and gudgeon-pin bearings were modified, and extra jets directed oil into the pistons (which had also been changed) for additional cooling.

A further modification was needed to the gearbox to cope with the still greater torque, and the type 915 transmission (developed from the type 908 racing gearbox) was introduced with a three-piece instead of a barrel-type housing. Surprisingly, perhaps, a four-speed gearbox was standard for all models, with a five-speed as an option, though for the British market the importers standardized on five-speed transmissions for the 'E' and the 'S'. The 915 transmissions had one significant change in that first and second gears were now on one plane, while fifth and reverse were 'out on a limb' away to the right. This certainly simplified matters for town driving, when first gear was used a lot, and even the Porsche addicts, conservative by nature, had to admit that this was a better layout. A fairly strong spring action guided the lever from fifth back to fourth, and it didn't take much experience to get the hang of the new pattern.

Still in the quest for better weight distribution the oil tank was moved from the right-rear wheelarch to a position just behind the driver's door. A release catch was hidden away in the B-post pillar, and the tank had a flap opening similar to that for the fuel tank in the left-front wing. This modification only lasted a year, because all too often the filling station attendants would mistake this for the fuel filler and fill the oil tank with benzine, often with

During 1970, a most successful year for Porsche at Zuffenhausen, the company manufactured its 150,000th car, which was purchased by David Nurse, a founder member of the Porsche Club of America. Ferdinand 'Butzi' Porsche, grandson of the firm's founder and designer of the 911's body, drinks a toast with Mr and Mrs Nurse.

disastrous results to the engine. The particular recognition point of a 911 made between autumn 1971 and autumn 1972, therefore, is the oil filler flap behind the right-hand door.

The oil tank was raised in specification to stainless-steel and increased in capacity, enabling Porsche to become the first company in the world to announce 20,000-kilometre (12,000-mile) service intervals. For a long time Porsche maintained a lead in this area, though some other manufacturers are now extending their service intervals similarly. The change to stainless-steel was necessary because the oxidation of oil tends to corrode the tanks from inside (damage is not usually caused by stone chips, as is often assumed), and the life of the previous oil tanks was sometimes as little as three years. Stainless-steel tanks will normally last at least six years, but they are certainly expensive, and a replacement tank will last longer if the oil is changed annually, even if the mileage is below 12,000. Also improving the specification, the door sills were made of Thyssen zinc-coated steel, which was virtually corrosion-free.

As the engine got bigger, the car became easier to drive, and longevity of materials was now a major consideration, so the clientèle began to change a little. No longer was the Porsche 911 merely a car for the enthusiast — it was becoming a rich man's toy as well. But rich men like their comfort, hence the introduction of air conditioning as an option, better heating and ventilation . . . and better suspension, too. For the 1972 model year softer Boge dampers were fitted all round, those at the rear with revised and more inclined mounting points, though Bilstein or Koni dampers could be ordered at extra cost. Only the 911S had anti-roll bars as

With the increase in engine capacity to 2.4 litres in August 1971 (E-programme) compression ratios were lowered and all models switched to regular-grade fuel.

A front air dam became standard equipment for the 911S in August 1971, and optional for other models. This substantially reduced the lift at high speeds, and the air dam was soon to be fitted to all models. With the power output increased to 190 bhp in 2.4-litre form, the 911S now had a top speed of 147 mph with acceleration to match. Note that the bumper overriders have now been dropped for the S model.

standard equipment, 15 mm in diameter both front and rear.

Aerodynamics were playing an increasingly important rôle on the race tracks. Porsche had started experimenting with trim tabs on the 907 and 908 racing cars some three years before and recognized the immense value of apparently innocuous pieces of aluminium tacked on to the front wheelarches. Indeed, a driver had died at the Nurburgring in 1970 when one of the tabs was knocked off his 908 and the car simply flipped over on to its back at high speed, in a straight line; from that point on research into aerodynamics intensified in the quest for greater stability and safety. The first product of this work was the air dam introduced for the 911S model, the first production car in the world to be equipped with something which is now commonplace, even among really mundane family cars.

The 911S now had a top speed of well over 140 mph, and the air dam was soon recognized as one of the most significant improvements ever seen on this model. At top speed the front of the car felt glued to the road, the steering was more responsive, and the car was not buffetted around to anything like the same extent when trucks were overtaken on an *autobahn*. All the air dam did, in effect, was to clean up the airflow underneath the car, thus reducing the lift from 183 pounds at maximum speed to 102 pounds, a 'something for nothing' factor which, apart from anything else, made the car less prone to aquaplaning on wet roads. Though standard for the 'S', the air dam was available optionally for the 'T' and the 'E', and such was the demand that it soon became standard equipment for all three versions.

The 911T was still fitted as standard with 5½J × 15-inch steel wheels with 165-section HR tyres, though 185-section tyres were available for the same rims. Alternatively, the 'T' could be fitted with the 6J × 15-inch enamelled steel wheels and 185/70 VR tyres specified for the 911E. For the 911S, 6J × 15-inch forged-alloy wheels with 185/70 VR tyres were standard equipment.

Although 1971 was another exciting model year it was a far from happy time for Porsche generally. Inflation was beginning to be felt across the world, and the Deutschemark-to-dollar exchange rate was worsening rapidly. So while labour costs at the factory rose sharply following a three-week strike (the first in the company's history), materials costs also rose, and demand slumped in the United States.

In the whole of 1971 Porsche produced just 11,715 cars, of which 357 were six-cylinder 914s, and the turnover dropped sharply from 420 DM million to just 315 DM million. Of the total production, the 911T accounted for 65 per cent, the 911E 15 per cent and the 911S 17.3 per cent, but the proportion of Targas had risen sharply to 44 per cent.

This was the first crisis point in Porsche's history, or at least the first real one since those early days, and it didn't suit a rapidly growing company which had been in the habit of doubling its turnover every five years or so. During that difficult winter short-time working was introduced, so that workers were laid off for about one day a week on average.

As though that was not enough, the management of the company was going through a crisis as well. Nepotism is the name given to the malady, for at the head of every department there was a Porsche or a Piëch. The sons and nephews of Dr Ferry Porsche were jostling for positions of power, in the words of Dr Porsche 'like sand in a well oiled machine', while some very talented people below them felt stifled and frustrated by what they saw. Dr Porsche saw the problems all too well, so he called the family together and explained matters as he saw them.

Furthermore, Dr Porsche had his way, and during the winter of 1971-72 some enormous changes were implemented. Heinz Branitzki, just 41 years old, was made financial director and Dr Ernst Fuhrmann, designer of the Carrera engine, was wooed back from the Goetze piston company to become technical director and spokesman for the board. Karlernst Kalkbrenner was appointed manager of personnel, and Dipl Ing Helmuth Bott was put in charge of development work. A new supervisory board was organized with Dr Porsche and his sister, Louise Piëch, at the head.

Each side of the family had four children, who became shareholders, and the five members of each family were each allocated 10 per cent of the company shareholding which, in an average year, is worth a dividend share of 500,000 DM apiece. Most of this, however, is traditionally ploughed back into the company, as are the working profits, to pay for the developments and expansions as they are needed. In exchange for this deal, the sons and nephews had to agree to leave their places in the company and branch out on their own, which they all did successfully.

Once into 1972 the reconstituted company began to forge ahead once more, and after a slow start the annual sales picked up to a total of 14,503, which was beginning to look respectable again. By now the pace of design was accelerating on two completely new projects — cars that became known later as the 924 and the 928. The 924, in fact, was being designed by Porsche at the behest of Volkswagen, as early clay models indicate, as a top model for VW-Audi which would replace the 914. Although VW opted out of the project at the height of the oil crisis, in 1974, they had good reason to be grateful to Porsche for continuing with the design solo and having it produced in Audi's Neckarsulm plant, which would otherwise have been closed down, perhaps permanently, during the recession.

The 928, on the other hand, was Porsche's own project, initiated in 1970 by Ferry Porsche, who could see that future

For the F-programme in 1972 all models had a larger, 85-litre fuel tank (not least because fuel consumption had deteriorated with greater engine capacity and lower compression ratios). The 'Space-saver' spare wheel became standard equipment using a collapsible tyre, and with it came an electric pump which plugged into the cigar lighter for energy. At this time, new ATS pressure-cast wheels were fitted to the 911E and became an option for the 911T.

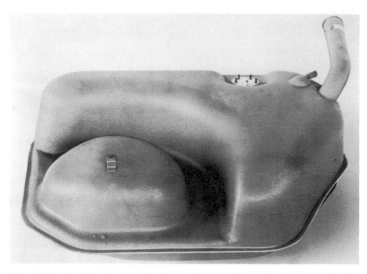

The 85-litre fuel tank comprises two steel pressings, the upper one being more complex in order to accommodate the spare wheel. The tank is lead-lined and pvc-coated.

American regulations would eventually demand a power unit larger but 'cleaner' than the six-cylinder could ever be. So, while the top brains at Porsche were thinking far ahead, work continued on more imminent versions of the 911.

One result of inflation was a sharp rise in prices, between 10 and 15 per cent depending on the model. Thus the 2.4-litre 911T rose from 19,969 DM to 22,980 DM, the 'E' from 24,975 to 25,980 DM and the 'S' from 27,140 DM to no less than 30,680 DM, thus passing the psychological 30,000 DM barrier that management had been worrying about.

Results for 1972 prove that the prices were just about acceptable, and of course the customers were now getting a lot of performance for their money. The 130-horsepower 911T had a top speed of 127 mph and would accelerate from rest to 60 mph

in a little under 10 seconds. If that was not enough, the 911E with 155 horsepower would reach 60 mph in around 8.9 seconds and go on to a top speed of 135 mph. The ultimate 911S, with 190 horsepower, would reach 60 mph from rest in 7.0 seconds and attain a maximum of 145 mph, rewarding the driver with a most exhilarating thump in the back when the rev-counter passed 4,000 rpm, and a mechanical induction howl which defies description, but is sheer music to the Porsche *afficianado*.

None of this character was spoiled in the minor revisions announced in the autumn of 1972, for the 1973 model. As mentioned, the oil tank was moved back to its original position, and in addition to the stainless-steel tank a completely stainless-steel exhaust system was introduced. Again, this is an expensive item when it comes up for replacement, especially if new heat-exchangers are required, but it should last at least six years.

A new 80-litre (17.6-gallon) fuel tank was installed, the extra capacity being achieved by adopting the Goodrich Space-saver collapsible spare tyre on a steel rim. This tyre has a cross-ply construction which collapses inwards when deflated, and is some two inches greater in diameter than the rim on which it is mounted. An electrically operated compressor pump is part of the kit, and this simply plugs into the cigar lighter to power the pump, which inflates the tyre to its correct pressure and diameter in a couple of minutes.

Two possible drawbacks are the installation in the laden car of the punctured wheel (though a plastic bag is thoughtfully provided to keep the dirty or wet tyre away from luggage), and the fact that the Space-saver is illegal in Britain, where regulations expressly prohibit the mixing of radial and bias-ply tyres on the same axle.

Minor revisions for 1973 included simplifying the serpentine oil-cooler in the front right wheelarch to make it less fragile, and specifying black plastic for the front horn grilles and the rear lamp surrounds. Engine internals were modified with reinforcement in the main-bearing area, while the 911E was fitted with new ATS pressure-cast wheels, which were available optionally for the 911T.

CHAPTER 6

Return of the Carrera

2.7-litre and 3-litre pacesetters

The name 'Carrera' was first used by Porsche in 1956 for the most powerful model in the 356 range, and it recalled a famous class victory by the German make in the Carrera Panamericana Mexico two years previously. The word is Spanish for 'race', and the Panamericana event was the daddy of them all, involving road racing, usually on dirt roads, from the north to the south frontiers of Mexico. After two previous attempts, Porsche succeeded in winning the 1,600-cc class in 1954, actually the last time the race was run, when Hans Herrmann finished third overall behind the big Ferraris of Umberto Maglioli and Phil Hill, averaging no less than 99.3 mph.

On and off the Carrera designation was given to the fastest Porsche in the range, and after the best of a decade it was allotted to a new model introduced at the end of 1972. Overnight this became a most sought-after car, though production was strictly limited for homologation purposes, based as it was on the 911S bodyshell.

The capacity of the engine was lifted to 2,687 cc by increasing the bore from 84 to 90 mm, the stroke remaining at 70.4 mm, and with the retention of mechanical fuel-injection the power output was increased to 210 bhp at 6,300 rpm. Stripped out to a bare 900 kilogrammes, the Carrera RS had amazing performance, accelerating from rest to 60 mph in under 6.0 seconds, and comfortably reaching 150 mph.

It was, of course, intended as a competitions car, and plans were laid to build 500 examples for homologation into the Group 4 Special GT category, though in fact a total of 1,600 Carreras were to be built so that the car could be homologated into Group 3. Of these, 1,036 were lightweights, and some 600 had normal 911S road trim installed after production. Just 100 Carreras were imported to Britain in 1973.

Experience had previously shown that the normal six-cylinder engine could not be bored out beyond 87.5 mm without getting dangerously near the limit, so to produce the Carrera engine Porsche eliminated the Biral cylinder inserts altogether. Instead they relied on a process which their engineers had perfected with the 917 power unit two years previously, using nickel-silicon carbide (Nikasil) to coat the aluminium cylinder walls. Although only a fraction of a millimetre in depth, this Nikasil process almost entirely eliminated wear and actually reduced the friction, thus finding a little more power.

Other than the capacity increase the power unit was identical to that of the 911S, including the cylinder-heads. It had around 10 per cent more power than the 'S', but no less than 18 per cent more torque, necessitating the use of a heavier clutch spring. The rev limit was increased to 7,300 rpm, and with a tremendous rush of power coming in at 4,000 rpm it was by far the most exciting road car produced by Porsche to date. Indeed, even now, some six years later, a Carrera RS is the most sought-after of all used 911 models, and a good example can fetch up to £10,000.

The Carrera was a distinctive-looking car on the road. For a start, the initial batch was produced in white with large red or blue script 'Carrera' side-winders on the sides, which couldn't fail to attract attention (usually unwelcome, from a Police officer). To complement the successful air-dam innovation of a year previously, the Carrera RS sported an upturned spoiler incorporated in the glass-fibre engine cover, usually referred to as a 'duck's tail' spoiler. At maximum speed this is even more effective aerodynamically than the air dam, reducing lift from 320 pounds to a mere 93 pounds, and dramatically improving the roadholding in fast curves. Also, it moved the centre of air pressure back by six inches, making the car even less sensitive to side winds.

Rear wheels on the Carrera were increased to seven-inches rim width, the front wheels remaining at six-inches, and to accommodate this the rear arches were slightly flared, by around two-inches. Heavier 18-mm anti-roll bars were fitted, and Bilstein dampers were specified.

There was, additionally, a competitions model called the RSR, which we'll come to later, of which 49 examples were built specially for track racing with around 305-309 horsepower and such items as twin-plug heads and type 917 racing brakes and with the weight stripped to the bare minimum.

The RS was so different from the 911S that it had to be built on a special line, not that that made any difference for homologation purposes providing the minimum number of 500 was produced,

and it is surprising that the model could be sold in Germany for as little as 33,000 DM. Every vestige of soundproofing and undercoating was left out, and rubber mats were put on the floor. The rear seats were missing, and the front seats were light, simple and firm, but nicely shaped and still comfortable.

Interior trim was standardized in matt black, and luxuries like a glove-box lid, door trim, coathooks and even the front compartment counterweight spring, were dispensed with. The rear engine cover was made of glass-fibre, and was secured by rubber straps.

The net effect was to reduce the weight of the car to 900 kilogrammes (1,984 pounds), and to endow it with a fearsome turn of speed. As well as the improvement in acceleration, however, it could corner at 0.912g, aided by the wider rear wheels and the aerodynamic appendages, thus becoming the fastest cornering Porsche ever produced for road purposes. Yet the type 911/83, as it was designated, was still entirely reasonable for road use, and it still ran on 91-octane fuel! In its first year, 1973, the

The Carrera model is perhaps the most sought-after 911. The initial batch, all painted white with red or blue side-winders, had the first 210 bhp 2.7-litre engines with mechanical fuel-injection, would top 150 mph, and had exceptionally good roadholding. The ducktail spoiler, together with the front air dam, virtually cancelled lift at top speed.

Carrera RSR model became synonymous with success, sweeping up three international and seven national championships. The most creditable of these was Peter Gregg's success in America, winning both the Trans-Am and the IMSA GT championships. Without doubt, though, the most remarkable single success of the Carrera was outright victory in the 1973 Targa Florio, after the failure of the prototype Alfa Romeo team to go the distance. Gijs van Lennep and Herbert Mueller went on to take a splendid victory, the first for many years to go to a 'production' car, and perhaps it was fitting that a 911 Carrera should have won in Sicily that particular year, for pressures by the Grand Prix drivers on the CSI resulted in a permit for the Little Madonie mountain circuit being withdrawn, so ending a great classic event.

Production of the Carrera continued in 1974, though in rather more prosaic form. The mechanical injection system continued to be fitted on the 2.7-litre engine, which still developed 210 bhp, but the car itself was fully 'productionized' with all the comfort fittings of the 911 series, and in the process perhaps it lost a little of its appeal to the true enthusiast. The distinctive duck's-tail spoiler was removed from the normal specification, and the RS

appelation dropped, though for the British market the spoiler was kept until 1975.

For the 1974 model year the 911 series moved on yet again, as the G-series (the eighth evolution in ten years). The most notable mechanical improvement was the general adoption of the 2.7-litre engine with Bosch K-Jetronic fuel-injection for the 911 and 911S while the 'T' and 'E' models disappeared. However, the mechanical injection system on the Carrera failed to meet the increasingly strict American emission standards, and was consequently withdrawn from that market.

The K-Jetronic system was far more efficient, drawing precisely measured quantities of petrol into the induction system at a rate determined by the airflow. Fuel burning was as efficient as modern technology allowed, and with other aids for America the 911 continued to meet US standards without difficulty. As a by-product, the engine became notably more economical, and would typically cover an extra three or four miles per gallon. Also, of course, the 911 showed useful gains in power and torque with the adoption of the 2.7-litre engine, and became a much more relaxing car to drive in everyday conditions.

Another view of the Carrera, clearly aimed at the American market. The engine cover was made of glass-fibre, and aluminium was used extensively to reduce weight.

Alongside the Carrera model, the 911 T, E and S versions continued with 2.4-litre engines. The horn grilles and air intake in the engine cover were now painted matt black.

The G-programme Porsches announced in the summer of 1973 signalled another major forward step. The 2.7-litre engine was standardized, and Bosch K-Jetronic injection was installed on the 911 and 911S (note that the T and E models were dropped). This helped significantly to reduce exhaust emissions through better combustion, but the Carrera RS continued with mechanical injection. Collapsible bumper bars were now fitted.

The collapsible bumpers, designed with withstand parking knocks, were mounted on a tubular alloy framework which would crumple progressively in an accident exceeding 5 mph. Optionally, these bumpers could be mounted on hydraulic recoil dampers which would withstand and recover from heavier impacts. A red reflective 'Porsche' strip was now featured at the rear.

In 2.7-litre form the basic model now had 150 horsepower, and a top speed of around 133 mph. The 911S, now rated at 175 horsepower, had the advantage of a higher compression ratio (8.5:1 against 8.0:1, though it still consumed 2-star petrol), as well as bigger inlet and exhaust pipes, larger-diameter ports, larger valves and different camshaft timing.

Visually, the G-series range was identified by the new aluminium bumper bars, with thick rubber protectors and different types of mounting. As standard the bumpers were located by collapsible alloy tubes, which would absorb low-speed knocks, but needed replacing after an accident. Optionally (but standard for Britain) the bumpers had shock-absorbing backing so that they would recover from a minor impact without damage. In both cases, they had flexible concertina fairings to the wings.

A new, simpler one-piece front anti-roll bar became standard, 16 mm in diameter on the 911 and 911S and 20 mm in diameter

on the Carrera; the bar was now rubber-jointed to the wishbones and pivoted in rubber bushes carried by the front cross-member. At the rear, fabricated-steel semi-trailing arms were replaced by lighter, stronger alloy forgings which contained larger-diameter rear wheel bearings.

All cars were now fitted with the front air dam, whilst the new rear bumpers dictated a new exhaust silencer with a different tail-pipe location. Later in the model year the heat exchangers (which duct air from the hot exhaust for interior heating) were aluminized, to increase greatly their life expectation.

Within the fuel-filler neck is the orifice to the windscreen washer reservoir, now boasting a capacity of nine litres (two gallons). Most owners fail to realise that two litres of anti-freeze is recommended per fill — the average sachet is far from sufficient — and frozen washers are the inevitable penalty.

That year Porsche reverted to the single 12-volt battery, mounted in the luggage area, due to the new bumper-bar shape at the front. The bumpers themselves were now protected by thick rubber strips, and the rear number plates were flanked by heavy (but still stylish) rubber pads which would absorb parking knocks.

Car interiors were extensively revised, notably with the adoption of lighter seats with built-in headrests. Even on the standard 911 these were very comfortable and well-designed, but an optional 'sport' seat with more hip wrap-round was available at extra cost. The Targa models (imported to Britain with right-hand drive only since October 1972) were given a better one-piece roof location with a central locating peg, while the Carrera now had electrically operated windows, in line with the rest of the 911 range.

The G-series cars were fitted with inertia-reel seat belts as standard, and adjustable side-window demisting vents were installed at the extreme ends of the facia. The steering wheels were given large protective pads, those on the 911 and 911S being 15.75-inch diameter, compared with 15-inch on the Carrera. Facia knobs and switches were also changed for crash safety, while the door trims were redesigned to incorporate rigid pockets with hinged covers, which doubled as armrests. The tachometer was now electronically operated, a quartz-electric clock was specified, and there was some tidying-up as regards the location of fuses and relays, and the positioning of auxiliary lights.

Driving comfort was improved a little, too, with the adoption of

The horn grilles disappeared from the front of the G-series 911 range with the introduction of collapsible bumpers. Turn indicator lights were now recessed into the front bumpers, while heavy rubber pads protected the rear end.

an over-centre spring for the clutch pedal, and to lighten the braking effort, the brake pedal was increased in length from 9.1 to 9.8 inches to give more leverage. The Carrera retained the alloy 'S' calipers in the brake system, while the lower-powered models used the smaller M-type cast-iron calipers.

It is typical in Porsche's history that competition cars are the forerunners of production models, so it is appropriate to mention here the evolution of the full 3-litre RSR model which was built for the 1974 customer-racing season. Whilst the engineers at Weissach were busy developing turbocharged production engines (to which we'll refer at greater length later on) they took one more step — the final stage, in fact — in the development of the basic

911. The objective was to wring a little more power out of the Carrera RS, but the obstacle was the limitation of cylinder-wall thickness. Porsche's solution was to revert from magnesium to pure alloy for the die-cast crankcase, which was heavier but more rigid, and this enabled the engineers to adopt the 95 mm Nikasil-coated bore that was necessary (in conjunction with the 70.4 mm stroke) to achieve a 3-litre capacity.

As it was an evolution of the Group 3 Carrera RS, it was necessary to build only 100 cars for the 1974 season, ostensibly road cars, but the records show that a total of 109 cars were built, 49 of them as pure racers and the remainder with some road trim. Discounting the Turbos which followed, these Carrera RS and

RSR 3.0 models were, if you like, the ultimate 911s with full race performance available 'off the shelf'.

Those built specifically as road cars now developed 230 horsepower, though it's interesting to note that they were little, if any faster than the 2.7, despite having 10 per cent more engine capacity and power. This is almost certainly due to the greater frontal area, for in this form the RS had 917-type brakes, eight-inch rims at the front with nine-inch rims at the rear, further extensions to the wheelarch flares, and a full-depth air dam compensated by a larger rear wing. The catalogue weight was 900 kg (1,984 lb), which might have been a little optimistic.

The RS had a fairly exotic specification, the engine now being fitted as standard with a racing crankshaft and con-rods and a lighter flywheel. Though more expensive to buy than the RS 2.7, it was less expensive to convert to full-race RSR trim, as were most of them.

By comparison, the RSR was initially a little disappointing, for the power output was 'only' 315 bhp at 8,000 rpm, but the

The familiar flat-six engine is beginning to look overwhelmed by the apparatus of the Bosch K-Jetronic injection introduced in 1973, but it did lead to smoother running, improved economy and lower emissions. This is a 'fully laden' American-specification engine featuring an air pump (left of cooling fan), catalytic converter (bottom left) and exhaust gas recirculation.

Also new in 1973 were the 'tombstone' high-back driving seats, designed to provide head restraint in a rear-end accident.

change from throttle butterflies to slides restored the more usual 110 bhp/litre and power went up to 330 horsepower. The car was never raced by the factory in this form, but it scored numerous victories for privateers in 1974 and 1975, including the European GT Championship in both years.

Few modifications were announced to the 911 range in the summer of 1974 for the 1975 model year. Among the detail changes, the heating system was improved both as regards adjustments and consistency, and fresh-air ventilation was increased. The aluminized heat-exchangers were reduced in size, and a heater fan boosted the volume of air at low road speeds. Also, there were now two (red) heater control levers, one each side of the central handbrake, enabling the driver and passenger to alter the volume of air to the footwells individually.

Alternators were uprated to 980 Watts to cope with the power demands of standard and optional equipment, which included electric windows, two-stage heating for the rear window, and of course the heater fan, all of which could combine on a cold day to put a great strain on the electrical system. Also, of course, an electrically operated sunroof was available as an option.

For the 911S, third and fourth gear ratios in the type 915/16 box were raised, and fourth and fifth ratios were raised in the optional 915/06 five-speed box, to give more relaxed high-speed driving.

The 3-litre Turbo model (type 930) was announced at the Paris motor show in October 1974, going into limited production in 1975 chiefly as an homologation exercise in readiness for the new Appendix J competition regulations coming into force in 1976.

Front and rear aluminium bumpers on collapsible or recoil mountings were featured on the 1974 models.

A special run of 500 911s was made in 1974 to celebrate the Porsche company's 25th anniversary in manufacturing.

The factory prepared the way to build the required 400 cars, but the demand for this lavishly equipped model surprised even the most optimistic men in the marketing department, and the Turbo was soon promoted to the position of 'flagship' of the range.

The Turbo's 3-litre die-cast alloy block was the basis of the Carrera 3 model announced in the summer of 1975 for the 1976 model year, replacing the 911S. The range was now standardized with Bosch K-Jetronic petrol-injection, and although the Carrera's power output dropped slightly to 200 horsepower it was a great deal more flexible than its mechanically injected predecessor, developing a healthy 190 lb ft of torque at 4,200 rpm, which made it a particularly flexible and pleasant road car. At this point, therefore, the range was simplified with the 2.7-litre 911, the 3-litre Carrera 3 and the 260 bhp, 3-litre Turbo.

The range had now reached another evolutionary stage known as the I-series, the most significant feature being the use of fully rust-proofed steel for the body as well as the chassis. The chassis itself had been made of Thyssen steel for two years, successfully (as far as anyone could tell after this period) combating the rust menace, and now the body, too, would be made of the same steel, zinc-coated on both sides and offered with a fully comprehensive

ATS pressure-cast alloy wheels were standardized for the 911 in 1974, with 6J x 15 rims and the same 185/70 VR tyres as on the 911S.

six-year 'Longlife' warranty against corrosion. Soundproofing was improved at this point with a thicker layer of insulation on the rear bulkhead.

Although the 911S was now dropped, the 911 model virtually took over with the same engine, though now rated at 165 horsepower (compared with 150 bhp previously for the 911, and 175 bhp for the S). Unlike the Carrera and the Turbo, Nikasil coating for the cylinder-liners had given way to the cheaper but still effective Alusil coating initially developed in America for the Chevrolet Vega power unit.

With an 8.5:1 compression (and still using 2-star fuel) the 911 proved a potent machine with 165 bhp, virtually as quick as the former S version. Despite having an increasingly full complement of luxury equipment, it still weighed in at 1,120 kilogrammes (2,468 pounds) and had a very useful turn of performance: from rest to 60 mph in 7.2 seconds, to 100 mph in 18.8 seconds, and a top speed of 138 mph.

The Carrera 3, as it had become known, had a still higher level of equipment, which didn't cause the performance to suffer. With a full 200 horsepower at its disposal in 1976, this model would accelerate from rest to 60 mph in 6.0 seconds, to 100 mph in 15.2 seconds, and had a top speed of 145 mph.

By the summer of 1975 (1976 models) the galvanized chassis had been in production for a couple of years, and now the entire body shell was made of Thyssen double-sided hot galvanized steel, which was almost impervious to rusting. This bare, unpainted Targa chassis has stood outside the Weissach office block for nine years to date without any sign of deterioration.

An improved interior temperature control was incorporated on the 3-litre Carrera model in 1975, involving a temperature dial between the seats and automatic sensors in the cabin.

Remote control for the electrically operated and heated exterior rear-view mirror was another feature of the 1976 model Carrera 3. The mirror stem is pivotal, and the backing is matched to the colour of the car.

The Turbo is dealt with in the next chapter, but for purposes of comparison this was tested by *Autocar* in September 1975 and gave the following figures: zero to 60 mph in 6.1 seconds, to 100 mph in 14.5 seconds, and a maximum speed of 153 mph. The slower acceleration time to 60 mph is easily explained, because the ultra-wide Pirelli P7 tyres endowed the car with such grip that they refused to spin. If the tester used too many revs to start, the clutch would slip; too few, and the engine lost its urge and took time to build up to 3,000 rpm when the turbocharger would become effective. Even so, the 8.4-seconds increment from 60 to 100 mph is quite astonishing, a true yardstick of the phenomenal acceleration for which the Turbo is noted.

Although the model range was looking better than ever, with the high-volume 924 model to be announced later in the year, Zuffenhausen was in a period of gloom with low demand and production rates following in the wake of the Yom Kippur war and the first oil crisis. From the 'high' of 1973 when over 15,400 cars had been produced by Porsche, volume had slumped to 11,624 in 1974 and again to 9,710 in 1975, though by the year-end demand was on the upturn again. As usual, the American market was dictating the pace, though for once a slack European market was being felt.

The Carrera 3 Targa, now with the 'black look' finish dispensing with chromework completely, became one of Porsche's most popular models worldwide, offering marvellous performance with convertible appeal.

Even better interior equipment was installed in 1976 (1977 model) on the Carrera 3. Standard equipment included radio speaker installations in the doors, anti-theft door-locking knobs in the lining, electrically operated windows, electric mirror and deep pile carpet.

As well as the unique anti-corrosion guarantee offered by Porsche in the 1976 models, there were other refinements for the ever more discriminating customers to enjoy. The Carrera and Turbo models, for instance, had a new automatic heating control replacing the two rather rudimentary levers in the 911. The thermostatically controlled automatic system enabled the driver to dial his required level of cooling or warmth, from zero to ten, on a small dial between the seats, and a thermostat with twin sensors inside the car would make constant adjustments to the outlet valves.

Another innovation, aimed particularly at the American market, was the optional Tempostat device, or cruise control, which would keep the car going at any chosen steady speed on a motorway. This was controlled by pulses from the electronic speedometer, and was uncannily effective in maintaining legal speeds without stress. The Tempostat could, of course, be cancelled immediately by accelerating, braking, or simply by the driver flicking the lever down. Moving the lever upwards would call on the Tempostat to bring the car back to its former cruising speed.

There were a couple of mechanical improvements to be noted on the 1976 models. Firstly, the oil-pressure pump was uprated to increase the oil flow through the engine, and secondly, the engine cooling fan was changed from 11 to just five blades, driven at a higher speed, to increase the alternator output at lower engine speeds. The 80-litre (17.6-gallon) petrol tank was now lead-lined

In June 1977 Dr Ferry Porsche presided over a celebration of the quarter-millionth Porsche manufactured, naturally enough a 911. The white car was lined up alongside the first 356 made in 1948.

to prevent internal corrosion, and the fuel pump was moved to the front of the car to combat vapour lock.

On the 911 model, better hot starting was obtained by fitting a supplementary air slide between the intake pipes of numbers 5 and 6 cylinders, and this model was also revised in having its front suspension struts inclined inwards at a greater angle to facilitate camber-adjustment. The car was also given the later A-type cast-iron front brake calipers, with the same pad area as the S-type calipers used on the Turbo.

Standard transmission equipment was now the four-speed type 915/49 gearbox, the 915/44 five-speed or 925/09/12/13 three-speed Sportomatic being optional — limited-slip differentials were also available to order, as before. It was felt that with the increased torque of the 2.7 and 3.0-litre engines a four-speed box was perfectly adequate (indeed, the Turbo's bigger and stronger gearbox was only available as a four-speed), though the British market ordered exclusively the five-speed gearbox as standard equipment as the Porsches had now firmly established themselves in the up-market sector.

The 1977 model-year cars announced during summer 1976 had little in the way of novelties. The type 915 gearbox underwent alterations, notably to the first and second ratios, which were fitted with twin baulking segments, while the first-gear dogs were cut asymmetrically to facilitate engagement from rest.

Such was the demand for Porsches among thieves, the factory introduced a new type of door-locking mechanism involving a

57

The Carrera 3 was dropped midway through 1977, and was replaced by the 3-litre 911SC, which incorporated all the luxury features of the Carrera — automatic heating control, flared arches, pile carpet, electric windows and so on. With a bigger crankshaft and larger main bearings, the 3-litre engine now developed 180 horsepower — less than the Carrera by 20 bhp, but with better torque characteristics.

small knurled wheel in the door lining, and shorter buttons, which disappeared into the lining when the door was locked. This made life a little harder for the more amateurish thieves, who had found ways of hooking the knob upwards, but of course technology improves on the wrong side of the law as well! At this point, too, pivoting quarterlights were omitted from the Targa models.

For left-hand-drive markets a brake servo was announced for the Sportomatic versions of the 911, an innovation which could not be expected to meet with enthusiasm from the purists, but was considered not only acceptable, but desirable by the customers who favoured semi-automatic transmission.

It was another year before the servo was fitted on all versions, including right-hand-drive models for the British market, but any market resistance to this brake assistance was soon quelled. The servo was not a super-light device which would stand the car on its nose, American-style, but was rather an unobtrusive aid to braking, which came in particularly handy when the brakes were cold, and at low speeds — times when the 911 models had previously felt rather unresponsive.

In the summer of 1977, for the 1978 model year, a number of significant revisions were made to the range. The Carrera and the 2.7-litre 911 were dropped in favour of a single 911 model, the 3-litre 911 SC. At the same time the Turbo model went up in capacity to 3.3 litres and no less than 300 horsepower. By now the 924-model production was in full swing, giving Porsche another bite at the 2-litre market which it had long since vacated, while the 4.5-litre 928 model had been announced and was due to go into production.

Although the name 'Carrera' disappeared for the time being, the car lived on. The new 911 SC had exactly the same mechanical components, including the wider wheels, flared arches, automatic heating control and so on.

The 3-litre engine was slightly detuned to 180 horsepower, compared with 200 bhp for the Carrera and 165 for the former 911 version, but with the new camshafts the torque curve was actually higher and flatter than that of the Carrera, making the car much more flexible to drive, and virtually as fast in any type of road condition.

Alterations to the power unit for the 911 SC included a new, stronger crankshaft with larger-diameter main and connecting-rod bearings. The crankcase, as before, was made of die-cast alloy with Nikasil cylinder-liner treatment, and the cooling fan reverted to 11 blades in order to reduce the noise level. Contactless capacity-discharge ignition was adopted, reducing maintenance requirements, and an air pump became standard worldwide in order to reduce the pollution level (this partly accounts for the lower power output from an otherwise substantially similar engine).

The brake servo became standard equipment, with the single disadvantage that it slightly reduced the luggage capacity where it's most needed, in the deepest and widest part of the

Interior of the 911SC (equipped with Sportomatic transmission, to be phased-out mid-1979). the **380 mm** steering wheel, thick-rimmed and leather-trimmed, had by now become small enough to partially obscure the speedometer.

compartment.

One modification that a Porsche-phile would notice straight away was the adoption of a Porsche-designed clutch-disc hub which eliminated the gear chatter always present when the engine was 'hunting' at low speeds. The five-speed gearbox became standard equipment, and the auxiliary over-centre spring assist for the clutch was carried forward from the Carrera to the SC.

No changes were announced for the 911 SC in 1978, but in 1979 (for the 1980 model year) the ignition timing was 'optimized' (to quote the engineers) and the power went up to 188 bhp. The main reason was to improve the fuel consumption by around 10 per cent in response to the second fuel crisis, and in line with American demands for more economical cars, and still the engine would run on regular-grade fuel. Quietly and without any fuss, the Sportomatic transmission was dropped from production.

Just prior to the announcement of the 1978 model range the 250,000th Porsche, a 2.7-litre 911, had rolled off the line with suitable ceremony. The figure may be a drop in the ocean to any other manufacturer, but every Porsche is a hand-made precision

Another classic, the 911SC Targa, photographed in 1979 against a rural background in Britain.

instrument and general standards hardly apply. The total, which includes racing cars, was achieved in 28 years, and rather surprisingly excluded all the 125,000 914 models — even those with Porsche six-cylinder engines — which were deemed to have been made by another company, VW-Porsche.

In 1979 demand was stronger than ever, the breakdown showing around 11,000 911 SC models produced, 5,000 928s at the same plant in Zuffenhausen, and some 23,000 924s at Neckarsulm. It was part of Professor Dr Fuhrmann's plan that the 911 model would quietly be run down when the 944 model was launched in 1981, and buried with the advent of the 944 Turbo planned for 1984 (but deferred for 12 months). Dr Ferry Porsche was deeply concerned about this and relationships between the two men grew strained, due too to the development of the 928 model without full reference to the Supervisory Board headed by Dr Porsche, and in December 1980 it was announced that Professor Fuhrmann would retire, to lecture at the University of Vienna. His place was taken by Peter W. Schutz, a naturalized American from the board of the Klockner-Humbolt-Deutz diesel company.

Fully versed by Dr Porsche, Peter Schutz knew exactly where his priorities lay. Plans to simplify the specification of the 928 (in the language of the marketing men, or 'cheapen' according to others) in order to overlap the 911 were scrapped, the V8 model being developed henceforth as a more spacious, more luxurious and faster 'business man's express'.

Further developments of the 911 model proceeded apace. For the 1981 model year the power was raised from 188 to 204 bhp by means of increasing the compression ratio and 'optimizing' the ignition and Bosch K-Jetronic settings, to use the delightful word first heard at Weissach and since adopted by other manufacturers! The 911's maximum speed rose to 146 mph and acceleration times were usefully improved, and to appease the conservationists there was a very substantial improvement in fuel economy.

Since August 1971, and the introduction of the 2.4-litre models, the six-cylinder engine had been weaned to a diet of 92-octane fuel, low on lead emissions but rather uneconomic on account of the low compressions. Raising the compression ratio to 9.8:1 now meant a reversion to 98-octane fuel, but the savings were out of proportion, 21 per cent overall it was claimed. In the urban cycle the consumption improved from 16.33 mpg to 21.08 mpg, and in overall terms the owner could reliably expect better

Comparison of a 1965 2.0-litre 911 (left) with a 1984 3.2-litre 911 Carrera reveals the subtle but important evolution in the outward appearance to cope with both changing legislation and the performance increase brought about by adding, in round figures, another 100 bhp.

The 911 Cabriolet was seen in definitive form at the Geneva Show in March 1982 and went into production a few weeks later. This is the Sport version for the British market with Turbo-style wheels and rear wing.

than 20 miles per gallon.

A surprising exhibit at the Frankfurt Show in September 1981 (nine months after Peter Schutz took office) had the Porsche world buzzing: a 911 Turbo 'Studie' with four-wheel drive *and* a cabriolet convertible top was an ideas prototype, not destined for production in that form, but an expression that the management was continuing to invest in technical development for the model, and that new versions could be expected. Mounted on a mirror floor so that the workings could be seen, the project car had a drive-shaft running forward from the gearbox, through the tunnel that usually housed the linkage, to a 924 Turbo differential between the front wheels. The 'Studie' was a runner, but had

nothing so sophisticated as a centre differential, merely showing off a concept that was to be developed further.

The Porsche company had more to celebrate, for it was the 50th anniversary of the founding of Ferdinand Porsche's design consultancy in Stuttgart, and in that month of September the Zuffenhausen plant produced both the 200,000th 911 model and its 300,000th car. The annual report showed that in a difficult trading year the turnover was down by 5.6 per cent at 1,165 DM million, but profit was maintained at 10 DM million, while the workforce was virtually unchanged at 4,906. Production was slightly down at 28,000 cars, but overall sales were up to 31,500, due to de-stocking in America.

One of the most exciting developments in the 911's history was the Carrera model, announced with 231 bhp in 1983. Searing performance, yet with good fuel economy, was the theme. The Targa version illustrated has the standard, 928-style alloy wheels, the Cabriolet the optional Fuchs wheels with black centres and polished rims.

It took the company only another six months to bring the cabriolet concept to readiness with the unveiling of the 911 SC Cabrio at the Geneva Show early in 1982, with full production about three months away. There was nothing revolutionary about the idea, which could have taken shape at any time since the Targa model was introduced in 1966, since basically the cabriolet was a Targa with the roll-over hoop deleted. Some judicious strengthening was carried out to the floorpan, and despite the efforts of the BB company Porsche continued to insist that the Turbo couldn't be offered as a Targa or cabriolet since the power and torque of the engine would be too much for the weakened bodyshell.

The roof was not power-operated, but involved a clever cantilever mechanism that made it easy to operate and ensured that, with the roof installed, it was taut, quiet and weatherproof. The rear window could be unzipped, not so much as a fresh-air feature as to ensure that the plastic window would not be scratched or folded when the roof was stowed away.

Chassis number information contained in the appendix material shows up a feature that surprised many at the factory (though not all, by any means). In the first full year of production 4,277 cabriolets were produced compared with 2,752 Targas, while in the 1984 model year, and following the introduction of the Carrera model, the roles were reversed: 3,793 Targas were made and only 3,103 cabriolets, the full convertible losing ground both in Europe and in America. Many people bought them for their novelty value, of course, and may not have been ready for a change within 24 months, but the cabriolet did not sweep the Targa away as some people expected. As a matter of interest, the records show that in the 1983 model year 12,728 911s were made in three forms, plus 1,080 Turbos, while the following year 13,482 911s were made and only 881 Turbos, the turbocharged model losing ground as the 911 Carrera substantially closed the performance gap.

Here we are getting ahead of ourselves, though. Before the 1983 model year production started, some very minor changes were

A rare combination of 911 options was built for the Swedish Motor Show in 1985. The Carrera Cabriolet was supplied with the M-491 'Turbo look' bodywork, with wheel arch extensions, wheel spacers, and type 930 suspension and brakes, then topped off with the expensive aluminium detachable hardtop.

announced for the 911 SC, including a new primary silencer (muffler) to reduce the noise and exhaust emissions, the Swiss market in particular stiffening up its regulations. The heater system emergency override lever situated between the seats was thankfully deleted. The heating and ventilation system is fully automatic, and any stranger who asked: 'What's this?' and pulled the red lever would damage the mechanism, which needed a workshop repair. Provision was made for static rear seat belts and the radio system was given four interior speakers; further changes were made to the Turbo, dealt with in the next chapter.

The Carrera returns

For a model that brought the 911 close to the performance of the Turbo, it was inevitable that the Carrera name should be revived, not denoting a special version this time, but a normal production car. The Weissach technicians claimed that 80 per cent of the engine was new, though it was developed from existing components, most notably the alloy engine block, which retained its 95 mm bore. By adopting the Turbo's crankshaft, though, the stroke was increased to 74.4 mm and the capacity was taken out to 3,164 cc, by this and other means increasing the power substantially from 204 bhp to 231 bhp at the same engine speed of 5,900 rpm. The torque curve also benefited, rising from 180 lb ft at 4,200 rpm to 209 lb ft at 4,800 rpm. New pistons with higher domes increased the compression ratio from 9.8 to 10.3:1, and not only was the performance level raised but fuel economy benefited too, in a way that owners could only regard as miraculous!

Further reference to the appendix material at the end of this edition shows what progress had been made in 20 years, but the two prime examples are illustrated in this way (both sets of figures are from *Motor* magazine):

| Year | Model | Acceleration | | Maximum | Overall mpg |
		0-60 mph	0-100 mph	speed	(Imperial)
1965	911 2.0 (130 bhp)	8.7	24.1	130	21.1
1984	911 Carrera 3.2 (231 bhp)	5.3	13.6	152	21.1

Another 1.2 litres, another 100 horsepower, and the acceleration figures are improved dramatically; the maximum speed rises by 22 mph, yet the fuel consumption remains exactly the same. The overall concept of the 911 has changed not at all, the bodywork is almost identical but, being the tireless engineers that they are, the Weissach staff have worked unceasingly to develop the running gear throughout the 21 years that the car has been with us.

There are a great many features on the Carrera model that need pointing out. The Bosch K-Jetronic system was replaced by Bosch's Digital Motor Electronics (DME) system which, like Motronic, maps out the ignition and injection requirements taking all the variables into account: throttle opening, ambient and engine temperatures, engine loading, engine speed and battery voltage. The control box is placed under the driver's seat, yet another example of finding a home for something that wasn't envisaged when the car was designed (look at the facia for further examples!), and DME also has a fuel shut-off when the car is coasting, a further fuel-saving measure.

Within the engine bay there are more features to describe. Attached to the Turbo's crankshaft is a new flywheel with calibrated pickups for the DME system. The Turbo's cylinder-head seals are adopted in place of regular gaskets, and the inlet and exhaust valves are increased in diameter by 2 mm. The inlet manifold is new, and so too is the exhaust system.

Owners will be interested to know that the latest type of timing chain tensioner, 930.105.058.03, can be retro-fitted. This item has been a veritable Achilles' heel of the 911 ever since it came out, but after umpteen modifications (almost one every year) the engineers really do believe they have cracked the problem of breakages which may lead to expensive engine failures. The tensioner now receives oil from the engine's lubrication system rather than having its own reservoir, and is a completely new design. Until now these tensioners have always been at the back of owners' minds, especially with older cars, and if the new design works properly it's a problem that can be forgotten about. Finally, so far as the engine is concerned, the alternator capacity was increased from 75 to 92 amperes.

The brakes, gearbox and body also benefited from improvements. The brake discs were increased in thickness by 3.5 mm, still ventilated all round of course, and the pressure limiting valve from the 928S was incorporated in the system to reduce the proneness of the front wheels to lock up on wet roads. Also, the Turbo model's eight-inch servo was fitted instead of the previous seven-inch unit.

In the transmission, fourth and fifth gears were raised to suit the extra performance, and an external oil cooler was fitted to the gearbox, newly designated type 915/67. As you'd expect the acceleration is now absolutely vivid, and in practice second gear now feels rather 'short' as the engine is bouncing on the rev-limiter in a remarkably short time. At higher speeds the Carrera performs in each gear like its predecessor did one ratio lower. It does not have the raw muscle of the Turbo at low engine speeds, to be honest, but it's remarkably flexible and does make the Turbo look something of a luxury now.

As a special option the Carrera is also available with the Turbo's body and suspension, including the widely flared arches (which actually lower the maximum speed!), interior fitments and perforated disc brakes. The standard models benefit from improved interior heating, adopting twin boost fans to the footwells from the Turbo's specification, the sunroof option features an improved wind deflector, and the Targa has improved weather sealing. Visually, the Carrera models are distinguished by having pierced alloy wheels similar to those on the early 928 models (goodbye, sadly, to the distinctive Fuchs wheel as standard equipment, though still available as an option), fog lights are incorporated in the front apron, the Carrera badge is proudly attached to the engine cover, and American versions also have an upshift indicator within the tachometer.

The Carrera model was received with considerable enthusiasm, needless to say, and in the year when Professor Fuhrmann planned to phase the model out it reached a new peak of popularity, the 14,000-plus examples built not setting a record, as it happens, but being among the best years' figures on record.

All this activity in the autumn of 1983 could hardly be replayed a year later, but some worthwhile improvements were announced for the 1985 model year. The seats were improved without spoiling their qualities, the backrests being made 40 mm higher (though further increasing the feeling of claustrophobia in the back, unfortunately). The height and rake of the seats was now controlled electrically, though the old-fashioned lever remained for reach, and seat heating became available optionally. Safety belt latches were now attached to the seats, making them easier to locate.

Central locking became an optional item (standard on the Turbo), the windscreen washer nozzles were electrically heated to combat winter freezes, the gear lever was shortened in length to allow faster gear-changing, and finally, the radio antenna was deleted, replaced by an element in the windscreen. It is almost completely invisible, and is said to maintain the reception performance throughout the life of the car.

Production of the quarter-millionth 911 is now well in sight, in the first part of 1986 probably, and bells will ring out in the province of Baden-Württemburg! Schwabian efficiency is something they like to talk about in Stuttgart, both at Porsche and across the city at Daimler-Benz, and this seems to be epitomized by the Porsche 911 model, still the heart and soul of the Porsche company.

CHAPTER 7

The 930 Turbo

A 911 in all but name

For two decades Porsche had played the Cinderella role in motor racing, going to Le Mans each year with cars of less than 2-litres capacity and playing second fiddle to Ferrari, Mercedes-Benz, Aston Martin, Jaguar and Ford in turn. Not until 1968, when the 3-litre 908 model came along, did this picture change, and the 5-litre 917 really greeted a new era. At last Porsche could pitch confidently for outright victories, having learned that 'big is best'.

It took only two years for the FIA to outlaw the 917s, which must go down in history as among the giants of endurance racing, and Porsche then turned its attention fully to the Can-Am scene into which Jo Siffert had broken with the 917PA. There, the 8.1-litre Chevrolet-powered McLarens were dominant, but Porsche got to work with turbocharged versions of the 917 flat-12 engine with tremendous success. Eventually the 917/30 developed up to 1,000 horsepower (the engineers even saw 1,200 bhp on the test bench) and it was described by Brian Redman as 'the ultimate racing car' — ultimate, not only because of its sheer power, but because of the intolerable strains it placed on the driver under acceleration, braking and cornering. To drive this car for any length of time, said Redman, a man really needed to be wearing a g-suit, for after 20 minutes the human body was sickened and weakened by the stresses imposed on it.

The Porsches of the Penske team swept to a resounding Can-Am victory in 1972 (George Follmer) and again in 1973 (Mark Donohue), crushing the dispirited McLaren team, but then the fuel crisis of 1974 ended this era just as certainly as the FIA had ended the 5-litre class two years before. Circumstances forced Porsche to take a fresh look at the World Championship for endurance racing, where the 3-litre RSR had performed reasonably well against the prototypes and had picked up some useful outright victories.

Foremost in Porsche's new strategy was the premise that a new FIA Appendix J set of rules would be introduced in 1976. Essentially, the more important World Championship for Manufacturers would be based on production cars, and the somewhat secondary World Sportscar Championship would cater for up-to-3-litre prototypes.

In March 1974 a completely new concept in endurance racing made its debut at the Le Mans trials, the Porsche 911 Carrera Turbo. Still basically the RSR that had served so well, the engine capacity was reduced to 2,142 cc so that when the FIA's multiplication factor of 1.4 (for supercharged or turbocharged engines) was applied, the capacity would not exceed the 3-litre unsupercharged limit for prototypes. The standard 2-litre crankshaft was adopted in order to reduce the stroke to 66 mm, titanium con-rods from the Carrera 6 were installed, and the bore was reduced to 83 mm.

With a single exhaust-driven KKK (Kuhnle, Kopp and Kausch) turbocharger, Bosch mechanical petrol-injection and a modest 6.5:1 compression ratio, the Carrera Turbo engine with 1.4 bar of boost developed 516 bhp at 7,600 rpm. Allowing for the FIA's rather rough-and-ready 1.4 multiplication, and assuming this to be a 3-litre engine, it therefore developed 172 bhp/litre compared with the RSR's 105 bhp/litre and the flat-12 Can-Am engine's 200 bhp/litre.

The Achilles heel of this machine was to be its type 915 five-speed gearbox, which was just not suitable for 406 lb ft of torque, and the failure of the fifth-gear pinion at Le Mans denied the car a possible victory in 1974; however, it finished second to the Matra-Simca V12, and so honour was partially satisfied.

So the stage was set for the addition of a sensational model to the Porsche range — the Turbo. At the Paris motor show, in October 1974, a full 3-litre turbocharged version of the 911 model was announced, luxuriously equipped and easily capable of exceeding 155 mph in a straight line. Significantly, this had a new type 930 four-speed transmission, with wider gear teeth to cope with the torque loading, and the clutch was enlarged in diameter from 225 to 240 mm (9.5 inches). The model was known internally as the 930 Turbo, though the marketing department continued to refer to it as the 911 Turbo, while in America it was called the Turbo Carrera since the Carrera model as such had now been dropped over there.

In standard form the Turbo had air conditioning, electric windows, leather upholstery and all the luxury appointments that a discerning customer would look for, and the 67,850 DM price tag was almost double that of the 2.7-litre 911 (35,950 DM).

Though one or two sceptics thought that it looked too much like a normal 911 to warrant the purchase price, it really wasn't all that hard to see the differences at a glance. Most notable was the pronounced flaring of the wheelarches, partly to accommodate the seven-inch (front) and eight-inch (rear) forged-alloy 15-inch-diameter wheels, and partly to accommodate the much wider wheels and arch extensions planned for the new racing regulations in 1976. In fact, for normal road purposes the wheels were — and are — if anything too wide, and with the Turbo components fitted into a normal lower-drag Carrera body the top speed would be even higher.

A full air dam and a 'picnic tray' rear spoiler on the engine

The Turbo, the most powerful road car yet offered by Porsche. With the help of exhaust-driven turbocharging, well proven on race circuits, the power of the 3-litre engine was boosted to 260 horsepower in 1975. This car would reach 100 mph from rest in around 13 seconds, and attain 155 mph.

cover gave the car its own character, quite apart from providing all the necessary aerodynamic qualities for 150 mph motoring, reducing 397 pounds of lift to just 38 pounds, while twin fog lights were attached to the front below the bumper bar. The Targa body was deemed not stiff enough, so the only version was the coupé, with an electric sunroof.

Unlike the racing Turbo which preceded it and used coil springs at the rear, the 930 Turbo had the normal torsion-bar suspension, though with bigger cast-aluminium 'banana' trailing-arms at the rear and larger wheel bearings. The rear diagonal suspension arms were more rigid and pivoted around the same fulcrum points as the RSR's. Spacers were fitted further to increase the front and rear track, effectively filling out the wheelarches, and the MacPherson-strut front suspension was modified to provide some anti-dive characteristics.

In the prototype show car the 12-inch disc brakes were both ventilated and cross-drilled for better heat dispersion, but the cross-drilling did not go into production for another two years due to lack of development, and this was a possible weakness of the car in its original form.

The engine had the same 95 x 70.4 mm bore and stroke (2,994 cc) as the 3-litre RSR, again with Nikasil coatings on the cylinder walls. Forged-alloy pistons were fitted, but the camshafts were changed to type 930/51 and ran in four bearings. The compression ratio was lowered to 6.5:1, and with 0.8 bar of boost (12 psi) the theoretical overall compression ratio was as high as 11.7:1, and the 930 Turbo needed 97 octane fuel passing through the Bosch K-Jetronic system.

Power was quoted at 260 bhp at 5,500 rpm, and torque at 254 lb ft at 4,000 rpm. Various road tests published in 1975 had the standstill-to-100 mph acceleration figure at between 11.8 and 13 seconds, probably depending on how brutal the test driver was with the clutch when starting off ... it proved difficult to unstick the back wheels, especially due to the turbocharger characteristics, and in most cases the 60-mph acceleration time was slower than that of the Carrera.

Early cars certainly earned rave reviews, but with cautions about the turbocharger's habit of providing a rush of power from 3,000 rpm upwards. Below 3,000 rpm the power was comparatively modest, but on top of the torque curve at 4,000 rpm the performance was of the neck-bending variety normally

Heavily shrouded by auxiliary equipment, the compact flat-six power unit (type 930) is a marvel of ingenuity. The turbocharger is to the left of the exhaust silencer, bottom left.

expected in pure racing cars. Stopwatch figures therefore didn't tell the whole story — take the car out on to the open road, surge past a slow-moving truck in second gear, and the owner immediately realised that he had the most potent road car in the world! Certainly the Turbo needed to be treated with respect on wet roads, as not a few owners found to their cost when hustling through roundabouts with power applied.

All this was achieved with a minimum of fuss and noise. The

The 3-litre Turbo on test with *Motoring News* in 1976, at the Chobham test track. Amazingly fast in a straight line, the Turbo demanded respect when nearing its very high limit of cornering capability. Above all, it is an entirely relaxing, quiet and effortless machine for high-speed road work.

The Turbo was deliberately marketed as a luxury model. Standard equipment included full air-conditioning, a choice of upholstery and a radio set. There has never been a Targa version as maximum body stiffness was required.

turbocharger tends to muffle and reduce exhaust noise, and general sound levels were lower than in (or around) the ordinary 911. Within the car, occupants could just hear the high-pitched whistle of the turbocharger blade accelerating to 90,000 rpm, but otherwise the excitement was in the sensation of movement rather than noise. This was a car that always seemed to be travelling 20 mph slower than the speedometer indicated, and obeying speed limits required as much self-control as a rigorous diet! But above all it was a very safe car in experienced hands. Few drivers ever explored the limits; indeed on public roads the opportunities rarely arose, and within its limits the Turbo was absolutely superb, with tremendous reserves in the areas of performance, handling and braking.

It was intended to build 500 of these cars for homologation, but

the demand was such that production was actually stepped up and no fewer than 1,300 were built in the first 24 months, by which time the Turbo was referred to as the 'flagship' of the range. In time for the 1976 racing season two derivatives were announced, the Group 4 Porsche 934 (which ran with virtually all its luxury equipment, including electric windows) and the way-out Group 5 Porsche 935 — the suffix numbers denote the racing category, hence the distantly related 936 is the Group 6 car.

In common with the rest of the Porsche range, the Turbo was given a full six-year warranty against subframe corrosion from the beginning of 1975, along with a 12-month unlimited-mileage warranty. During the summer, when the 1976 models were announced, the Turbo was enhanced with an electrically operated (and heated) exterior rear-view mirror. Production was now

71

The so-called 'Martini Turbo' built specially for the British Motor Show at Earls Court in October 1976, was white with Martini livery stripes, and had a full leather interior with red and blue panels. A number of replicas were marketed.

If anything, the Turbo is 'over tyred' and has substantial flaring on the wheelarches for homologation purposes. Front wheels are forged-alloy 205-section, rear wheels 225-section (7J and 8J x 16) with Pirelli P7 tyres.

standardized on Pirelli's P7 tyres, 205/50 VR 15 at the front and 225/50 VR 15 at the rear, these having an ultra-low profile and a 50 per cent aspect ratio, meaning that they are half as tall as they are wide.

Without any announcement the engine was given more manageable characteristics with the incorporation of a by-pass valve in the turbocharger, preventing the sudden build-up of pressure. At the same time the boost was raised to 1 atmosphere (14.5 pounds), with the pressure building up more gently from 2,500 rpm, and the car became considerably easier to drive on slippery roads.

Outwardly, the most obvious change for the 1977 model was the adoption of 16-inch-diameter rims, following the example of the 934 and 935 racing cars, which had been given the taller rims in order to give the tyre a bigger footprint on the road; this also allowed larger brakes to be fitted, and more cooling air to circulate. The Pirelli tyres were now rated as 205/55 VR 16 front and 225/50 VR 16 rear, and their grip was so astonishing that it was hard to get wheelspin from rest even on dusty surfaces. The racing cars, of course, had sintered clutch linings, but even this specification was insufficient to get Jacky Ickx out of trouble at the start of the Silverstone six-hours race in 1976, though the tyres on his 935 were, of course, considerably wider slicks.

Mechanical improvements included twin fuel pumps of a new design, a modified pressurized fuel accumulator, and an electrical pressure sensor connected to a new boost gauge within the

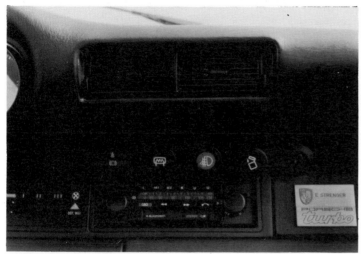

Better interior ventilation was seen in 1976 with two universally adjustable fresh-air vents at the centre of the facia.

tachometer. A brake servo was now included in the left-hand-drive specification, and the clutch pedal effort was reduced by fitting an over-centre auxiliary spring in the release mechanism. Detailed modifications were carried out on the synchromesh of the type 930 gearbox, while in the suspension the three-piece front anti-roll bar was replaced by a one-piece 20 mm bar, as on the 911. The rear trailing-arms were now of two-piece construction, with an eccentric screw adjustment, which made it easier to adjust the ride height.

Specification changes included the (optional) fitting of a rear-window wiper, a new rear window with two-stage heating (the windscreen had always been fitted with almost invisible heating elements), and a new centre console which carried cassette tapes, separate fresh-air and blower controls and centre outlets for the fresh air.

The Turbo moved into its second, final major form in 1977 for the 1978 model year, when the engine capacity was increased to 3,299 cc and an air-to-air inter-cooler was shoe-horned into the engine compartment in order to lower the temperature of air entering the engine via the turbocharger. These changes raised the power output substantially and at last the car was given the cross-drilled brakes and four-piston calipers identical to those originally fitted on the 917 racing car, and subsequently to the 935 'silhouette' car.

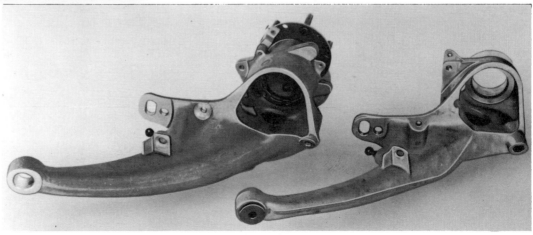

Cast-alloy 'bananas' — the rear semi-trailing arms — were first incorporated into the Porsche range on the Turbo, replacing steel pressings, with the advantages of lightness and strength. The Turbo part is on the left, 911 on the right.

Another 2 mm was squeezed out of the bore, while the stroke was increased to 74.4 mm, to find the larger capacity, and this entailed a new crankshaft, and larger main and connecting-rod bearings. In fact, it was virtually a new engine, for at the same time the compression ratio was increased to 7:1. Power increased by 15 per cent from 260 to 300 bhp at 5,500 rpm, while the torque went up by 20 per cent from 254 to 303 lb ft at 4,000 rpm.

A significant improvement in the transmission was the adoption of the Porsche-designed clutch-disc hub, which was more flexible than the previous design and eliminated the gear-teeth chatter which had always been a feature of the six-cylinder models. However, this new hub was bulkier than the previous design, and it meant moving the engine back by 30 mm (1.18 inches), though impairment of the handling was so slight that it really only showed up on a race track. To compensate for the greater bias to the rear, back tyre pressures were increased radically from 34 to 43 psi.

The air-to-air inter-cooler substantially reduced the temperature of the boosted air re-entering the engine, contributing to improved thermal efficiency, and this unit

A main feature of the Turbo 3.3-litre motor was the installation of an air-to-air inter-cooler fitting snugly under the engine cover, lowering induction air temperature and improving efficiency.

The rear hatch had to be extensively redesigned for the Turbo 3.3 to make room for the inter-cooler, and the rubber wing surround takes on a different (but no less efficient) shape.

replaced the air-conditioning radiator which had previously been under the grille in the engine cover, but was now removed to the nose of the car. An air pump became standard to clean the exhaust emissions, and the brake servo also became standard equipment for all markets.

By now the brakes were sensationally efficient, and they remained so no matter how hard the car was driven. *Motor* tested the car and found it would exceed 1.0g in braking from 30 mph with only 75 pounds pedal pressure, while it would exceed 0.9g in braking from 70 mph, pulling up in a mere 174 feet. The car also passed with ease the test of stopping 20 times from 100 mph at 45-second intervals without any signs of fading. Despite the servo, *Motor* reported that the brakes were a little heavy until they had warmed up, which at least dispelled any fears that the servo might somehow spoil the car.

According to *Motor* the Turbo 3.3 was the world's fastest-accelerating production car, reaching 60 mph from standstill in a mere 5.3 seconds and 100 mph in 12.3 seconds; 120 mph came up in 19.1 seconds (a respectable time for 100 mph in most high-performance cars), and the Turbo pressed on to a maximum speed of 160.1 mph. All this was achieved at 15.9 mpg overall, including performance runs, and the computed touring consumption was 18 mpg.

Just as impressive were the top-gear mid-range increments: 50 to 70 mph in 7.2 seconds; 60 to 80 mph in 6.0 seconds; 70 to 90 mph in 5.7 seconds; 80 to 100 mph in 6.1 seconds; 90 to 110 mph in 7.3 seconds, and 100 to 120 mph in 8.7 seconds.

About the only feature of the car not to merit an enthusiastic comment was the air conditioning, which might in any case have been below par on that particular car. *Motor's* summary says it all:

The Turbo 3.3 as sold on the British market shows off its classic features to advantage. Although manufactured 17 years after the 911's debut, the car certainly has nothing dated about its lines, a tribute to the quality of the original design.

'Its acceleration is simply breathtaking, and the maximum speed is very high, but the same may be said of a number of "supercars". Likewise, its astonishing roadholding and its powerful brakes are matched by a select few of the world's best motor cars, though none has the same astonishingly sensitive feel.

'The real achievement of the Turbo is its supreme practicality. It is as much at home dawdling along the High Street as it is flat-out on the *autobahn*. It can be treated like an ordinary everyday car, and indeed, there is nothing on the market at any price which has a longer interval between recommended services. In our opinion it is probably the best example of precision engineering on four wheels ... the most practical of supercars.'

No changes were announced for the 1980 model year, but at the end of the 1979 calendar year the Turbo was withdrawn from the American market for the usual reason — noise and exhaust emissions. The Turbo version rested on its laurels until the 1983 model year when, with faster versions of the 911 (Carrera) and the 928S in the pipeline it was given some significant modifications. More optimization, in Porsche's terms, included an improved warm-up regulator, a new fuel distributor with a capsule valve designed to improve full-throttle response, a new ignition distributor, and a new twin-tailpipe exhaust system which lowered the noise level without impairing the power.

Power output remained at 300 bhp, but the torque curve benefited, rising from 42 to 44 mkp (303 to 318 lb.ft) at the same engine speed of 4,000 rpm, and the Turbo proved to be measurably faster as a result. *Autocar*, which summed up the performance as 'amazing', lowered the standstill to 60 mph time to 5.1 seconds and the 100 mph time to 12.2 seconds, recording a mean average speed of 162 mph and a best of 165 mph.

The journal's standing-kilometre time of 24.5 seconds (with a terminal speed of 133 mph) was narrowly beaten the following year when John Morrison, a Porsche sales manager and racing driver, was timed officially at 23.985 seconds for the standing kilometre in a competition to establish the world's fastest-accelerating production car. A Lamborghini Countach, an Aston Martin Vantage and a Lotus Esprit Turbo were left behind in the event organized by the RAC Motor Sports Association.

Absolute performance isn't everything, and accompanying the slightly higher acceleration curve and improved drivability came a notably improved fuel consumption. In the urban cycle it was 29 per cent better at 18.22 mpg (previously 14.1 mpg), at a steady 56 mph it was worse at 29.12 mpg (34.9 mpg), while at a steady 75 mph it was better again at 23.94 mpg (18.5 mpg). Well, can anyone imagine a Porsche driver going along at a steady 56 mph?

In average driving the Turbo would now achieve 18 mpg normally, while a long journey at fairly legal speeds could easily see 20 mpg, a figure that wouldn't disappoint any owner. The interior heating, incidentally, was improved by fitting two extra fans to force air into the footwells (the Carrera model followed suit when it was announced a year later), and in 1984 the Turbo was equipped with the 928S model's central locking system, electrically-operated seats also joining the list of standard equipment.

The introduction of the M-491 'Turbo look' offered by the factory is likely to cause some confusion, since 231 bhp Carreras could be ordered with the flared arches, uprated suspension and brakes and wheel spacers. In the first year only the coupé body style was available, but from 1985 the cabriolet was also offered with the Turbo look, even though there isn't a Turbo cabriolet! An aluminium factory-supplied hardtop is also available for this version, styled exactly like a normal coupé roof but detachable, and suitably expensive at close on 10,000 DM.

The 959 advances technology
The curvaceous Gruppe B design study that appeared at the Frankfurt Show in September 1983 could hardly be recognized as a derivative of the 911 concept, but its basic elements were true to the type. The monocoque 911 body was intact, but now carried carbon-fibre and Kevlar sections at the front and rear that made it look like something out of 'Star Wars'. A full-width rear wing was integral to the design and the drag coefficient was lowered to just 0.32, around 10 points lower than a standard Turbo model and, painted in metallic pearl white, the show car was simply stunning.

In the tail, and mounted on a spaceframe, was a full 956-type racing engine taken out from 2.6 to 2.8 litres and rated at a nominal 400 bhp, clearly with very low boost. It had the water-cooled cylinder-heads and twin turbos of the racing car, and production examples in the future would have hydraulic valve lifters, it was said, together with one-piece siamesed cylinder barrels (still three per bank, of course) instead of individually cast

Breathtaking arrival on Porsche's stand at the Frankfurt Show in September 1983 was this Gruppe B design study, still 911-based though evolved almost beyond recognition. Its specification drew on the company's racing experience and promised new technological advances too.

barrels. At the heart, still, was the nominally air-cooled flat-six alloy engine, in common both with the Turbo road car and the type 956 racing cars.

Nor was this all. Advancing the 1981 show concept, the Gruppe B featured a brand-new six-speed gearbox and a very sophisticated four-wheel drive system, using an electronic control to vary the amount of drive going to the front wheels. An extra lever on the steering column could be used by the driver to vary the torque split for slippery conditions, Alpine roads or motorways, though technical director Helmuth Bott was reluctant to give more details. Later on we learned that a viscous

coupling is used in the centre differential, so adjusted that when the rear wheels start to spin the drive is gradually increased to the front wheels.

It was said at the time that the Gruppe B would be made in limited numbers, at least 200 for homologation, starting in the autumn of 1984 so that the Gruppe B could start its competitions life midway through 1985. At the time of writing, early in 1985, that programme has slipped back at least a year, due partly to the infamous metalworkers' strike and then to the technical difficulties in bringing the transmission to perfection. Production was now due to commence in April 1985 with the objective of

For the 1984 Paris-Dakar Rally, Porsche built three 911s incorporating elements of the Gruppe B project including four-wheel-drive, and one of them shows here that it is as much at home on Weissach snow as in the Sahara desert sands for which it was intended.

As it progressed towards production the Gruppe B design became known by its type number, 959, and acquired additional vents at front and rear to let cooling air in and out.

For the 1985 Paris-Dakar rally cars, 959-style bodywork, complete with full-width rear airfoil, was adopted. A Carrera engine provided 230 bhp and Kevlar and alloy panels kept weight to a minimum.

making the 200 examples within 12 months. The estimated price of each car is an overwhelming 420,000 DM for a road-going model, and more still for a 'luxury' version and a competitions version; the latter could, eventually, cost as much as a Porsche 956, which was quoted at 650,000 DM when customer versions became available!

For this money the customer expects only the best. The maximum speed will be over 180 mph and the Gruppe B will accelerate to 125 mph (200 km/h) in no more than 15.4 seconds. The car will ride on Dunlop Denloc tyres developed from the safety racing design, and there will be pressure sensors to tell the driver if one tyre is losing air.

Within three months the basic elements of the design were incorporated in three 911s destined for the Paris-Dakar Rally, a gruelling 12,000 km 'raid' across the deserts of Northern Africa taking 21 days. Jacky Ickx, who'd won the event in 1983 at the wheel of a Mercedes G-wagen, put together the 1984 team led by himself with actor Claude Brasseur, 1982 winner René Metge with Dominique Lemoyne, and Weissach technicians Roland

Kussmaul and Eric Lerner.

The four-wheel-drive transmissions were greatly simplified, using a mechanical centre differential lock, and featured the trusted five-speed transmission coupled to a 3-litre engine, normally aspirated and detuned to 225 bhp to cope with low-grade fuel. Ickx was unlucky to have his wiring loom burn out in the desert, Kussmaul being delayed while doing his job in effecting a temporary repair, and it was left to the Belgian race and rally driver Metge to storm away into the lead, which he held to the end. Ickx made up ground rapidly, recovering from 139th position to sixth at the end, while Kussmaul was placed 26th after putting his 911 into a spectacular roll in the desert.

A 100 per cent finishing record in this event, possibly now the toughest in the world, coupled with the outright victory, was a convincing demonstration of Weissach technology and not a bad demonstration for the 911, by now a 20-year-old design.

The Gruppe B design had been advanced by the time it was exhibited at the British Motor Show in October 1984, though it was still some way from production. A type number, 959, had been allocated to the Gruppe B and will surely be the reference of the future. The magnesium wheels were now 17 inches in diameter, and their 'spokes' were hollow and linked to the tyre pressure sensing devices, so that an impending wheel failure could be signalled. The suspension, using double wishbones front and rear and dual shock absorbers, had adjustments available to the driver to control both the ride height and the spring rate on the move, rather increasing his responsibilities!

As a result of wind-tunnel testing, louvres were now cut into the front and rear fenders, at the front to assist cooling of the water radiator and at the rear to aid the cooling of the turbochargers. A new design of KKK turbocharger was used to give good throttle response at low engine speeds, and Porsche announced that the 959's engine had been refined to meet new European regulations concerning exhaust emissions; they even expected it to be suitable for use with American-style catalysts!

In January 1985 Porsche went back to the Sahara, again with a three-car team in the Paris-Dakar 'raid', Jochen Mass replacing Kussmaul in the third car. This time the cars were designated Porsche 959s and used the six-speed gearbox, though again with the mechanical torque-splitter.

Visually the 959s bore a closer resemblance to the Gruppe B, with enclosed headlamps faired into the front wings, and the full-width rear airfoil. Kevlar materials were used for the external panels (and for the full-length undertray) though the doors and engine cover were made of aluminium. With a total of 270 litres in the tanks — 100 litres in the front and 170 litres in a container behind the seats — the cars had a range of about 1,000 kilometres in desert conditions. With a ground clearance of 290 mm (about 11½ inches) the Paris-Dakar cars were equipped for the worst terrain, though like the Gruppe B they featured dual control arms and double shock-absorbers all round.

Despite all the equipment on board they weighed only 1,190 kg without fuel, and the quoted top speed was 215 km/h (135 mph) at 6,000 rpm. This time the Carrera engine was installed, rated at 230 bhp when tuned to run on low-grade fuel.

The 1985 rally was not such a success for Rothmans-Porsche: Mass retired early after an accident, Ickx was eliminated when he hit a pile of rocks, hidden by sand, at high speed, and Metge went out with a broken oil pump at half-distance. They had not led the event, having been hoping to move up in the later stages, but they had the consolation that, at least, none of the new parts being tested had given any trouble.

Question marks remain over the future of the 959 as a Group B competition car. In the world of rallying such purpose-built machines as the Peugeot 205 Turbo 16, the Lancia Delta S4 and the Ford RS 200, virtually 'Formula 1' cars for off-road work, hold a theoretical advantage over any production-based car, no matter how powerful; and in Group B racing any advantage of four-wheel drive remains to be proved. Doubtless, the 959 will be a quantum leap ahead of the 911 Turbo and BMW M1 machines that contest the Group B category of the World Endurance Championship, and with as much as 650 bhp it ought to be clearly superior in lap times. It will, though, be ranged against Enzo Ferrari's fabulous GTO model, mid-engined, rear-driven and without question a production racing car of the future. The arrival of these two formidable contenders at Le Mans in 1986 is something that sports car enthusiasts will await with keen anticipation, for just as the 935/78 was a challenger to the 936 racing car, so the 959 Gruppe B could well be lapping at speeds not far from those of the 956s.

CHAPTER 8

The competition 911s

From 160 bhp 2-litre to 330 bhp 3.0 RS/RSR

Even the creators of the 911 model in the early-1960s could not have guessed that one day a derivative would develop over 700 horsepower, and earn an outright victory at Le Mans. But competitions are in Porsche's bloodstream, and the 911 was given its baptism in the 1965 Monte Carlo Rally merely four months after the model began to flow down the production line. At the time the competitions department was absorbed with the 904 and subsequent racing cars which were considered more suitable for track work, so it was only natural that engineers Herbert Linge and Peter Falk should choose the Monte for the newly homologated 911.

The power output was raised from 130 to 160 bhp by simple means: polished intake ports, increased compression ratio, different camshafts, revised carburation, platinum spark plugs, a lightened flywheel, and a through-flow exhaust system were all incorporated. The final-drive ratio was changed to lower the gearing, competition clutch linings were fitted, and a ZF limited-slip differential was installed. In the suspension department Boge front damper struts were fitted, then larger rear brake calipers were chosen, together with air scoops for the front brakes. The fuel tank was increased in capacity to 100 litres (22 gallons), and the car had all the usual equipment for rallying — seat belts, Tripmaster, grab handles, headrests, tool box and so on.

It is clear that a good deal of thought and effort went into the preparation of this car, and it paid off with an excellent fifth place overall in the final results after a trouble-free run in sometimes appallingly snowy conditions. Even more pleasing was the 911's victory in the Grand Touring class, the main object of the exercise, though the sensation of the event was Eugen Böhringer's

drive in the mid-engined 904 model to second place behind Timo Makinen's Mini-Cooper.

For the 1966 rally season German driver Gunther Klass campaigned a car to a similar specification with a good deal of success, ending the year as the European GT Rally Champion. On the way, he won the German Rally outright and won the GT class in the arduous Alpine Rally, while a lesser-known individual named Wallrabenstein won the Austrian Alpine Rally outright. On the hills, Eberhard Mahle earned the title of European GT Champion.

The announcement of the 911S midway through 1966 offered more scope for the private teams, and for the 1977 season the Porsche factory itself ran a limited rally programme with Vic Elford/David Stone driving. For their customers Porsche offered a Stage 1 rally kit consisting of different carburettor jets and chokes, which raised the power from 160 to 170 bhp, and a Stage 2 kit, which included a through-flow exhaust system and further increased the output to 175 bhp.

Porsche's first official rally programme proved every bit as successful as the factory had hoped, and while Elford/Stone became the European GT Rally Champions with the 911S, Polish driver Sobieslav Zasada became European Saloon Rally Champion driving a 911. Elford's outright victories included the Lyon-Charbonnières (in which Porsches also took the next three places), the Tulip Rally and the Geneva Rally, while Zasada, remarkably, walked off with the Austrian Alpine Rally and later on, in his own 911, the Argentinian Grand Prix. This was not, as the title suggests, a road race, but a 2,000-miles road rally over rugged terrain. Zasada's was the only Porsche among the 376

Fittingly, the 911's competitions debut was in the hands of Porsche factory engineers Herbert Linge and Peter Falk. With the car homologated less than three weeks previously, they took first place in the GT category and finished fifth overall in the 1965 Monte Carlo Rally.

One of the most remarkable victories by a 911 in the 1960s was that of Sobieslav Zasada with co-driver Dobrzanski in the 1967 long-distance Argentine Grand Prix. The Polish team, driving the sole Porsche among 376 entries, won the 2,050-mile event by a clear 15 minutes in a record time of 23½ hours.

starters, and its success was quite outstanding.

The 911S was also making its mark on the hills, where Anton Fischhaber became the new GT Champion, and on the race tracks, where the GT class in classic endurance races fell to Porsche at Sebring, Daytona, Spa, the Targa Florio and the Nurburgring — a wider variety of circuits, from the flat-out Daytona banking to the tortuous 60 mph-average Little Madonie circuit, is hard to imagine, and sports enthusiasts were beginning to take a great deal of notice of the 911. But then, that's exactly what Porsche had intended.

By the middle of 1967 Porsche had a new weapon in the armoury, the 911R (for racing). This model, of which only 22 were built, was substantially lightened, utilized glass-fibre doors, front wings and engine cover, thinner windscreen glass and plastic side windows, and most of the 'optional' equipment, such as sound-proofing, heating and the rear seats, was deleted. In this

Vic Elford was one of the factory's most successful drivers in the late-Sixties, his works contract being backed by a successful bid in the British Touring Car Championship in 1967 with a 911T entered by A.F.N. Limited. In the same year Elford was the European Rally Champion at the wheel of a 911S.

Elford had a memorable duel with Jim Clark's Lotus Cortina at Brands Hatch in 1967; many people consider this to have been the heyday of saloon car racing.

way the weight of the car was reduced to a mere 800 kilogrammes (saving some 230 kg), while a prodigious power output of 210 bhp at 8,000 rpm was obtained by slipping in the Carrera 901/22 full-race engine, as originally seen in Maglioli's 1965 Targa Florio 904.

The factory retained three of these cars and sold another 19, though the 'production' examples gained a bit of weight and turned the scales at 830 kg. The first of the three works cars was given its debut outing in the Marathon de la Route (now, remember, an 84-hour high-speed trial around the Nurburgring) in the hands of Vic Elford/Hans Herrmann/Jochen Neerpasch. Like another of the three factory Porsches it was fitted with four-

For the second year running a 911 won the Spa-Francorchamps 24-hours touring car race. In 1967 the winners were Gaban/Pedro, and here in 1968 the all-German team of Erwin Kremer, Helmut Kelleners and Willi Kauhsen were victorious.

speed Sportomatic transmission, and the 911R recorded a splendid victory in the Marathon to vindicate this choice and prove to the doubting Porsche customers that semi-automatic transmission actually worked.

Another notable success notched up by the 911R was the capture of a string of records on the Monza banked circuit. Rico Steinemann (who later became Porsche's competitions manager), Jo Siffert, Dieter Spoerry and Charles Vögele had intended to go record-breaking in a Porsche 906, but the attempt was abandoned when the shock absorbers proved unequal to the task. With literally no notice at all beyond a frenzied 'phone call, Porsche despatched a 911R to Monza, and it proceeded to capture records at 15,000 kilometres, 10,000 miles, 20,000 kilometres, 72 hours and 96 hours. Every record was within the span 130.01-to-130.50 miles per hour.

Even contemporaries found it difficult to follow the complexities of homologation during the 1960s, for it was possible to homologate different versions of the same car into different groups. Thus the 911 and 911L model were homologated into Group 2 Touring, while the 911T and 911S were homologated into the Group 3 (GT) category. Further complicating the issue was the FIA's approval of certain 'S' components (such as camshafts, Weber carburettors and pistons) for the Group 2 911/911L, raising the output from 130 to 160 horsepower, and of the 911S engine installation into the lighter 911T, which had been homologated with a simplified equipment specification at a mere 923 kg (2,038 pounds).

For three years, therefore, from 1967 to the end of 1969, Porsches abounded in just about any category you went to see on a Sunday afternoon. Touring car racing? 911/911L. GT racing? 911T. Prototype racing? 911R, plus of course the 906, 907, 908 and 910 racers which really brought competition cars within the

Approaching the peak of his career, Vic Elford won the 1968 Monte Carlo Rally with David Stone in this factory 2-litre 911T.

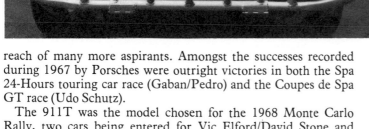

Laden with extra equipment, Sobieslav Zasada took part in the 1968 London-Sydney Marathon with this 911, but he failed to reach the finish.

reach of many more aspirants. Amongst the successes recorded during 1967 by Porsches were outright victories in both the Spa 24-Hours touring car race (Gaban/Pedro) and the Coupes de Spa GT race (Udo Schutz).

The 911T was the model chosen for the 1968 Monte Carlo Rally, two cars being entered for Vic Elford/David Stone and Pauli Toivonen/Tiuhkanen. The engines delivered 180 horsepower and the cars were geared down to 104 mph at 7,200 rpm in fifth gear — with the weight pared down to 2,350 pounds the performance was quite remarkable, and a 75 per cent limited-slip differential provided all the traction that was required to shoot up the icy cols. Elford and Toivonen secured first and second places overall in the Monte, then the most prestigious of all the world's great rallies. Up-and-coming Bjorn Waldegaard, with Lars Helmer, won the Swedish Rally the following month, but then it was Toivonen who won a series of events through the season to clinch the World Rally Championship for Porsche. Toivonen's tally included outright victories on the Geneva, East German, Danube, Spanish, German and San Remo rallies, surely

a record number of wins in one rally season.

1968 was Elford's year, too, the British driver recording one of the most amazing Targa Florio victories ever at the wheel of a 907 in May after collecting a puncture on his opening lap. Elford also made his Formula 1 debut that season in a Cooper-Maserati at Rouen, collecting sixth place and a championship point in the rain-soaked event. But above all it was the year of the Porsche 911, with first and second places in the Marathon de la Route

During 1967 Porsche built 20 of the ultra-light 911R racing versions, though the car was never homologated. It achieved tremendous success as a prototype, cracking endurance records at Monza and winning the Marathon de la Route in 1967, and again in 1969. The 911R was pared down to 830 kg.

On occasions the 911R was powered by the 230 horsepower 4-cam engine from the 906, but it proved remarkably inflexible for the road events that formed the R's main programme.

A dramatic action shot of Bjorn Waldegaard winning the 1969 Swedish Rally in his 911, a month after winning the Monte Carlo Rally.

(Herbert Linge/Dieter Glemser/Willi Kauhsen in the first car home), plus Grand Touring class victories at the Nurburg 1,000 Kms, Watkins Glen 6-Hours, Le Mans 24-Hours, Monza 1,000 Kms, Sebring 12-Hours and the Targa Florio. As icing on the cake, Erwin Kremer/Helmuth Kelleners/Willi Kauhsen won the Spa 24-Hours saloon car race for Porsche, so the directors could review the scoreboard at the year-end and claim 'game, set and match!'. All this was done, incidentally, without the help of the 911R, which could not be homologated as the Porsche company had decided against putting it into limited production purely for marketing reasons. It would, however, compete in occasional events for which prototypes were eligible, and sometimes it would win.

The 911T continued to be the mainstay of the 1969 rally programme, while a string of international race victories fell to the factory's 908 models (and the 917 at the end of the season in Austria). Bjorn Waldegaard, still with Lars Helmer, started the

For competition events in 1970 and 1971 the factory prepared lightweight versions of the 2.2-litre 911, designated the ST. The Rally version, developing 180 horsepower from the 2,195 cc engine, weighed 960 kg, while the racing version weighed 840 kg and had the engine bored out to 2,247 cc and developing 240 bhp.

Swedish driver Bjorn Waldegaard has been the most successful 911 rally driver, and is seen here winning the 1970 Monte Carlo Rally for the second time in succession (it was Porsche's third consecutive success).

Waldegaard went on to his second major success in 1970 in the Swedish Rally, held in February, again in a 911ST. It was also the second time running that he had won his home event.

The lightest 911 ever built; the 2.4-litre 911 ST driven by Gerard Larrousse on the 1970 Tour de France was stripped to an incredible 780 kg. It was powered by a 245 horsepower engine, and it finished second overall.

year in scintillating style with outright victories in the Monte Carlo and Swedish rallies, while Pauli Toivonen trounced the opposition in the rough and tough Acropolis Rally.

Guy Chasseuil and Claude Ballot-Lena, in their privately owned 911, won the Spa 24-Hours touring car race, where 911s took the top four places overall, and Grand Touring class wins were earned again at Daytona, Spa, the Nurburgring, Monza, Le Mans, the Targa Florio, and at Zeltweg.

In September 1969 the classic Tour de France event was revived, taking in 20 races, hill-climbs and road stages in six days. As prototypes were admitted, Porsche prepared a 911R for Gerard Larrousse and Maurice Gelin, and they duly won the event outright, with other Porsches being placed third, fourth and fifth. Larrousse went on to win the Tour de Corse with his 911R, repeating the previous year's victory of Vic Elford.

The competitions programme was given a boost with the announcement of the fuel-injected 2.2-litre 911, with its longer wheelbase, which would certainly come in handy both in rallies and races. A new Appendix J had now come into force barring the Porsches from saloon car racing ('and not before time, too', rivals

muttered), and the effort was concentrated on the 911S. Porsche could not be accused of missing many tricks, and the clever bit about the homologation of the 911S was the inclusion of twin-plug heads. Now freed from the 2-litre class limit, entrants could bore (but not stroke) an engine to the limit of its class, and in Porsche's case this generally meant increasing the bore by 52 cc to 2,247 cc and raising the power by 33 per cent from 180 to 240 horsepower. Rally versions were left virtually standard so far as the power units were concerned, but standard was generally enough.

Racing versions, known as the 911 ST, were really the forerunners of the Carrera, with thinner sheet steel used for the bodies in the areas of the roof and side panels, aluminium doors, and extensive use of glass-fibre for the bumpers, the luggage hood and wheelarch extensions. Plexiglass was used for all windows except the windscreen, and the ST was devoid of any luxuries like carpets, underseal, metal filling in the joints, passenger sun visor, glove locker lid and embellishments.

All this pared 180 kilogrammes off the weight, bringing it right down to 840 kg, and close to the 911R, on the scales. Two of

The car which shaped Porsche's competitions history for the mid-Seventies was the Carrera, in roadgoing RS trim on the left and in racing RSR trim on the right.

For events in 1972 Porsche made a series of lightened 2.5-litre 911s, with substantially flared wheelarches, wide wheels and front air dams. The engines developed 270 horsepower for racing.

The Carrera RS 2.7 was essentially a road-going car, developing 210 bhp with mechanical fuel injection. The car weighed 1,075 kg, and a total of 1,036 were produced. The 2.8-litre RSR, on the other hand, was given 300 horsepower and the weight was reduced to 900 kg. A total of 49 cars were built.

these devices were prepared for Bjorn Waldegaard/Lars Helmer and Gerard Larrousse/Maurice Gelin to use in the 1970 Monte Carlo Rally, and these crews duly obliged by finishing in first and second places, thus giving Porsche a coveted hat-trick of victories in this prestigious event. Driving a 'normal' 911S a month later, Waldegaard went on to score an unprecedented 'double-double' by winning the Swedish Rally outright for the second time.

Waldegaard's success in the Austrian Alpine Rally, coupled with Janger's victory in the Danube Rally and Claude Haldi's second place in the Lyon-Charbonnières event, enabled Porsche to claim the World Rally Championship in 1970. Linked with Porsche's crushing success in the World Championship for Makes in endurance racing, where the 917 and 908/3 models conquered all opposition, this success with catalogued road cars was enormously impressive.

Porsche's new research and development centre at Weissach had been in use for some two years now, first utilizing a circular asphalt pad on which steering characteristics could be checked; later on a number of other useful facilities were added. By 1972 the centre was fully operational, including a test track, pavé and water-splash sections, a cross-country course, and a number of test houses where tyre behaviour and engine development could be studied scientifically.

Since Professor Porsche had founded the company in 1930 the firm had always been a consultancy, and this aspect of Porsche's work accelerated in the 1970s. Weissach became the 'holy of holies', for the engineers had to safeguard not only their own development programme, but also various projects undertaken for other manufacturers, as well as the German and various foreign governments. These projects included road-building, motorcycle design, tanks and scout cars for military use, gearbox designs, and plans for complete cars. Apart from current racing-car development, the Weissach engineers under Dipl Ing Helmuth Bott were also working hard on turbocharging, on new Porsche racing designs, on 911 development, and on the design and development of the 924 and 928 models which came out during the 1970s.

Having detailed the rally successes, it must also be recorded that the Porsche 911 ST was an equally sure winner in the GT racing class, almost inevitably taking its category in the World

Championship long-distance races. It was common to find Porsche picking up eight or nine of the top ten points-scoring places in the 1,000-Kms and six-hours events, the 917s and 908s being backed up by the 911s, and the casual observer could have been forgiven for wondering what would happen to endurance racing if the name of Porsche disappeared overnight! Cynics would suggest that Porsche had frightened all the opposition away, and this criticism persisted through the 1970s, but it would surely be more accurate to say that Porsche did the job properly and the opposition failed to match up in the areas of development and production of customer cars.

Mention should be made of the lightest 911 ever built, a 911 ST for Gerard Larrousse to drive in the Tour de France. With the 'standard' ST weighing 840 kg, Larrousse offered the Weissach mechanics a case of champagne for every kilo under 800, and the resulting effort turned the scales at just 789 kg! The wings, as well as the doors and bumpers, were made of glass-fibre, and every non-functional component was removed. Many parts were drilled for lightness, and extensive use was made of titanium. Unusually, for Porsche, the Tour de France car ran on Minilite wheels. With twin three-choke Webers installed in place of injection, and a 70.4 mm-stroke crankshaft fitted to raise the capacity to 2,395 cc, the magnesium-block engine developed 245 bhp at 8,000 rpm.

But light and potent as this car was, it was no match for the Matra V12 prototype racing cars which finished first and second, pushing Larrousse down to third place overall. The glorious-sounding Matras had hardly been expected to finish this long-distance event, with its long road sections often covered in darkness, but the Velizy crewmen survived the ordeal surprisingly well.

With the fleet little Alpine-Renaults tipped for outright wins in 1971, Porsche reserved their main rally effort for the Safari Rally, encouraged by Zasada, who had competed previously as a private entrant. The standard 180 bhp engine was retained, though the gearbox had Monte Carlo ratios, allowing the cars a top speed of 112 mph. Suspensions were jacked up to their highest settings, giving the cars a rather unusual appearance, and of course the three team cars had all the usual 'extras' for what is perhaps the toughest road event in the world. The suspensions proved troublesome, Waldegaard retiring after leaving the road, and Ake Andersson going out after having rear-suspension problems. Zasada slipped from second to fifth place in the final stages with a misfiring engine, the trouble being traced later to a troublesome ignition master switch.

Later in the year Waldegaard finished second overall in the

Competition successes came quickly for the Porsche Carrera RSR. In 1973 Peter Gregg and Hurley Haywood won the Daytona 24-hours World Championship race outright after the frail 3-litre prototypes had retired from the event.

Fittingly, Porsche won the last Targa Florio race held on the Little Madonie road circuit in 1973. The triumphant car was the factory Carrera RSR in the hands of Herbert Mueller and Gijs van Lennep, which was run as a prototype with aerodynamic spoilers at the rear.

They even had one-make races for Porsches! In America, the second IROC (International Race of Champions) race at Riverside in 1973 pitted the best American and European drivers against each other. Mark Donohue won three out of the four races in the series.

RAC Rally, but that was the sum total of Porsche's rally achievements for the year. On the race tracks, of course, Porsche picked up their usual quota of GT class wins, including the Targa Florio, Monza, Spa, Le Mans, Nurburgring and Austrian events.

Another increase in standard capacity for 1972, to 2,341 cc, gave Porsche more scope for developing the competition cars, and the normal capacity for the racers was a bored-out 2,492 cc, at which size they developed 270 bhp. John Fitzpatrick, driving for Erwin Kremer, established himself as the leading Porsche driver for the year, winning the newly instituted European Grand Touring Car Championship and the richly endowed Porsche Cup. 'Fitz' won five of the nine qualifying rounds, while in the United States Hurley Haywood took the IMSA Camel GT Championship. There was disappointment, though, that the palmy days of rally victories had come to an end; Larrousse finished second in the Monte Carlo Rally, Waldegaard was second in the Swedish, and Zasada was second in the Safari.

Although Porsches were dominant in GT racing there was always the chance that another manufacturer would come along with something better — indeed Ferrari's Daytona looked good for the long-distance races and was to prove useful at Le Mans, while de Tomaso were also preparing for GT events. However, the Carrera RS, and the RSR racing version, were announced at the Paris motor show late in 1972 and were to prove the most successful of all Porsche's homologated cars.

In standard form the RS was not so different from the 911 ST that had gone before, although the capacity was raised to 2,687 cc with a 90 mm bore, and the standard power output was now 210 horsepower. The RSR, of which 49 were built, was the definitive racing version, and was rarely to be beaten in the next three years.

For the 1973 season the bore was enlarged by a further 2 mm and the capacity went up to 2,806 cc. The standard crankcase, crankshaft and con-rods were retained, but the four-bearing racing cams were installed and, as with the 911 ST, twin-plug heads were fitted. The power output was quoted at 'over 300 horsepower', and was generally reckoned on the factory cars as being 308/309 bhp according to the company's genial racing engineer/manager Norbert Singer.

For the RSR (racing) version the standard 980 kg weight of the RS was pared down to 900 kg, the car now having moved into a new, over-2.5-litre capacity class which required a minimum weight of that figure. Naturally this minimum weight caused Porsche no problems, though the car did gain weight with the wider racing wheels and the larger, type 917 disc-brake system which featured cross-drilling as well as the usual internal vents. A deep air dam at the front contained a larger oil-cooler, and mechanical fuel-injection was retained, instead of the Bosch Jetronic system fitted to the road cars.

As it happened de Tomaso did win two European GT rounds, development engineer Mike Parkes taking the honours at Imola and Clay Regazzoni at Hockenheim, but these races apart the remaining rounds were a Porsche benefit, and the championship resulted in a tie between Clemens Schickentanz and Claude Ballot-Lena. In America, Peter Gregg clinched both the Trans-Am series in competition with the more powerful GM Corvettes and Camaros, and the IMSA GT Championship.

Even more impressive were the outright victories in World Championship rounds, the first successes ever recorded by Porsche with production-based cars. Peter Gregg/Hurley

Haywood won the Daytona 24-Hours event after the rather frail prototypes had fallen by the wayside, and in Europe factory drivers Herbert Mueller/Gijs van Lennep won the last Targa Florio held on the Little Madonie circuit in Sicily.

For the 1974 season the competition 911s were taken one stage further with the introduction of a new 3-litre engine. For the RS, above, the new power unit developed 230 bhp, and for the RSR version, left, externally distinguished by vented wheel arches front and rear, it was uprated to 330 bhp. The result was a formidable contender in several racing categories.

John Fitzpatrick became the European GT Champion for the second time in 1974 at the wheel of Georg Loos' Carrera RSR 3.0. Loos, a wealthy German property owner, was a staunch campaigner of Porsches through the 1970s, and 'Fitz' was the most consistently successful GT driver through the decade.

Success in the Safari Rally eluded the factory again when the two 210-bhp Carreras entered for Waldegaard and Zasada encountered shock absorber problems that seemed endemic in the rear-engined Porsches over rough territory, and this, coupled with failures of the synchro rings in the gearboxes, led to the retirement of both cars.

Once the Targa Florio was out of the way Porsche's new policy, dictated by Dr Ernst Fuhrmann, became clear. At the Nurburgring 1,000-Kms the factory RSR had been considerably developed and turned into a Group 5 car, thereafter enabling customers to win the GT Group 4 class regularly. Through the years there has inevitably been some conflict of interest between Porsche's own programme and that of the company's customers, and generally Porsche has done the decent thing and, having proved a new model, moved on to new pastures.

The Group 5 car incorporated more of the 917's features, notably the wider wheels — 10.5 inches at the front, 15 inches at the rear — centre-lock titanium hubs, and (interestingly) coil springs augmenting the normal torsion-bar suspension. A huge,

faired-in wing distinguished the factory car, which had been reduced in weight to 820 kilogrammes with some fairly ruthless pruning. Mueller/van Lennep finished fifth overall at the Nurburgring, and followed this performance with a fourth overall at Le Mans behind the all-conquering Matra-Simca prototype team. At the season's end Porsche was placed third in the World Championship for Makes, behind Matra and Ferrari and ahead of the Gulf-Mirage team. Another good season for Porsche, though the writing was already on the wall for endurance racing!

Just one more development was in store for the normally aspirated Porsche 911 intended for competitions, and that was the enlargement of the engine to a full 3-litres (2,992 cc) in 1974. Basically very similar to the 2.7 RS, the 3.0 RS had the stronger aluminium crankcase with the bore taken out to 95 mm, throttle slides instead of butterflies, and a power of 230 bhp in standard (RS) form. A total of 109 cars were built, and of these 50 were uprated to RSR specification and 330 horsepower.

In the 1974 and 1975 seasons the RSRs won just about every category for which they were eligible, including the FIA GT

Championship and the IMSA Championship both years. Of all the 911 competition models the 3.0 RS/RSR must be regarded as the classic, and many are still competing regularly. As Dr Ferry Porsche remarked, if he'd known that the original 2-litre, 130-bhp engine could have been developed that far he would have suspected that its design was too robust and needlessly expensive to manufacture!

Before closing the chapter on the competition 911s, more words about the Safari Rally ... surely Porsche's biggest disappointment in the world of competitions. Bjorn Waldegaard went back for another try over Easter, 1974, and driving his standard-engined 2.7 RS was leading the event by miles until the car broke a drive-shaft during the last night. As this happened during a tropical storm it took ages for help to reach him, and the popular Swedish driver had to settle for second place overall.

It was four years before the Porsche factory attempted another rally, and sure enough it was the 1978 Safari. Two cars were entered for Waldegaard (released from his Ford contract for this one event), and for Vic Preston Junior, whose father runs one of the biggest car dealerships in Nairobi and is able to set up the best rally service plan of the Safari.

By now the 3-litre 911 SC engine was well developed, and a mechanically injected 250 horsepower version was dropped into a Carrera RS bodyshell, still complete with its duck-tail spoiler. The entire car weighed 1,180 kg.

The long lay-off from the world of rallying had not improved Porsche's chances of success, and both cars encountered suspension problems during the event. Preston, not accustomed to the Porsche, pluckily pressed on to finish in second place overall, while Waldegaard, who'd dropped as low as 13th early on, fought back desperately to finish fourth. The strikingly coloured Martini-Porsches were by no means disgraced, but Professor Fuhrmann's dream of winning the Safari seemed to have come to nought.

For some years thoughts of rallying lay dormant, inspiration coming from outside sources. In 1981, for instance, reigning

While in Monte Carlo to collect the 1978 Car of the Year Award for the Porsche 928 from Prince Rainier, Professor Fuhrmann and his team had the totally unexpected pleasure of welcoming Jean-Pierre Nicolas, winner of the Monte Carlo Rally in the Almeras-entered Porsche Carrera.

While Nicolas was upholding Porsche honour on the Monte, the factory was preparing a two-car attack on the Safari Rally. Waldegaard, hot favourite for the event, suffered suspension problems not unknown to Porsche on this gruelling route, and finished a very creditable fourth.

Vic Preston Jnr., finishing second overall, had his problems, too, but put in a steady drive to climb up the leader board.

Bernard Beguin pulled off a shock victory against works entries in the 1979 Tour d'Ypres, driving a 911 Carrera which was captured dramatically by Colin Taylor's camera.

Henri Toivonen testing the Rothmans team's 911 SC RS at the Weissach track in preparation for the 1984 European Rally Championship in which he and co-driver Ian Grindrod were to score some notable successes against formidable opposition.

The batch of 20 911 SC RS evolution cars lined up for inspection. This version, specifically developed for rallying, was homologated for the Rothmans Rally Team at the beginning of 1984.

World Rally Champion Walter Rohrl surprisingly found himself without drives (having signed for Daimler-Benz, who then had second thoughts about re-entering sport) and Juergen Barth lost no time in arranging a 924 Carrera GTS for the German driver. Rohrl competed in the Manx Rally that year in a Porsche 911, but retired with transmission failure.

Then, in 1983, the Rothmans company, Porsche's partners in endurance racing, decided to switch from uncompetitive Opels to Porsche 911s for the 1984 season, both in Europe and in the Middle East. Porsche would simply do the development work while the programme would be operated by Dave Richards at Silverstone.

Porsche built a special batch of 20 evolution cars, the 911 SC RS model, with a 3-litre flat-six engine rated at 255 bhp in the early part of the season, uprated to 290 bhp later on. The rally cars were equipped with Turbo brakes, and aluminium replaced steel for the front and rear bumpers, bonnet, engine cover, doors and front wings, the overall weight being reduced to 960 kg.

Following the success of René Metge in the Paris-Dakar event in January 1984 (described in the Turbo chapter) Henri Toivonen, son of former Porsche rally exponent Pauli, with Ian Grindrod won the Ypres 24-Hours rally, the Milles Pistes, the Costa Smeralda and the Madeira rallies, finishing the season as runners-up in the European Rally Championship. The programme might have been more successful still had Toivonen not missed some events due to a painful back injury.

In a parallel Middle East Championship programme, Saeed Al Hajri, from Qatar, and his British co-driver John Spiller fairly dominated the series to take the title, and then took part in the RAC Rally in November with Roger Clark as their team-mate. Against cars like the four-wheel-drive Quattros and Peugeot the Porsche 911 SC RS could hardly be a winner, but Roger Clark brought his car home in 11th place and Al Hajri, on his first event in the country, was 17th, both cars having been trouble-free.

The Rothmans-Porsche rally programme was to be scaled down in 1985 with Al Hajri competing in the Middle East events, Billy Coleman in Ireland and Bernard Beguin in France, none of them in the running therefore for the European Championship. It was to be a 'wait and see' year pending the arrival of the 959 as a homologated rally car in 1986.

CHAPTER 9

Turbos on the track

911 – 934 – 935 – 936 – 956 – 962

Having taken the important step into Group 5 midway through the 1973 season, Porsche took a still more important step forward the following year in preparation for the anticipated 'silhouette formula' which would herald the 1976 series — turbocharging was the key. At the Le Mans trials in March 1974 the Martini-Porsche wagon disgorged two striking Porsches, 911 derivatives which looked a little different and sounded unlike any 911 before. The muffled exhaust note, accompanied by a shrill whistle heard close-to as the car accelerated, announced the turbocharged version.

Competing as a prototype, the 911 Carrera Turbo, as it was designated, had to fall within a 3-litre capacity, and because of the FIA's equivalency rating of 1.4 for superchargers (or turbochargers) the swept volume of the flat-6 engine could not exceed 2,143 cc. Actually, by reverting to what was basically a 2.2-litre engine (with 83 instead of 84 mm bore, and the standard 66 mm stroke) the swept volume was a convenient 2,142 cc. It had a magnesium crankcase (changed to aluminium for Le Mans), a standard forged-steel crankshaft, but titanium type 906 con-rods and entirely new pistons and camshafts. The compression was reduced to a mere 6.5:1, and Bosch K-Jetronic injection was employed.

With a single KKK turbocharger installed, the engines gave upwards of 400 horsepower. The true power output depended almost entirely upon the boost pressure, which could be controlled by the driver by means of a knob inside the car. Early experiments had shown that the engine was prone to overheating, and one of the Le Mans trials cars had an air-to-air inter-cooler fitted, which seemed to cure the problem. By the time the car

competed in its first championship race, at Monza (where it finished fifth), the boost was 1.3 atmospheres, at which the engine developed 450 bhp, but later in the season 1.4 atmospheres and 470 bhp were seen regularly, with a reliable potential of 500 bhp at 1.5 atmospheres.

The cars had undergone some far-reaching changes under the skin. The fuel tank was removed to the interior, in the region of the back seats, and had to be cased in sheet aluminium to comply with safety regulations, while the oil tank was moved to the front of the car. Suspension was now fully coil-sprung, torsion-bars having been dispensed with, and the entire rear-end structure had been replaced by a simple spaceframe, with a fabricated alloy triangle replacing the trailing and diagonal arms. With extreme weight-saving measures, the 911 Turbo weighed a mere 750 kg.

Anyone accustomed to Porsche's standards would have been surprised by the unreliability of the two cars at Le Mans during the test weekend, when a pair of short races was held for the benefit of spectators, but it was the first public outing of a new concept — new for the 911, at any rate. Helmut Koinigg/Manfred Schurti retired in the first two-hours heat of the four-hours event with a broken rocker arm, while the van Lennep/Mueller car broke its turbocharger in the second, and various overheating problems had had to be overcome even before that. However, the cars proved capable of lapping the Sarthe in 3 min 55 secs, and were timed at 186 mph on the Mulsanne Straight.

Pitched against the Formula 1-powered Matra and Gulf-Mirage prototypes, which weighed under 700 kg and developed close on 480 horsepower, the four Turbo-Carreras built were clearly going to be outclassed. However, the programme was purely and simply

Whilst private teams enjoyed considerable success with normally aspirated 911s, the Porsche factory spent the 1974 season gaining experience with turbocharging. The car entered at Le Mans in June finished second overall to the winning Matra V12 prototype.

For most of the 1974 season Porsche ran two turbocharged Carrera RSRs, one for Van Lennep and Mueller and the second for Manfred Schurti (pictured at the Nurburgring's Karussel) and Helmut Koinigg.

Rear view of the 1974 turbocharged Carrera RSR, bearing only a passing resemblance to the 911.

Two views of the 2,142 cc flat-six engine with KKK turbocharging, developed for the factory's 1974 racing season. The smaller capacity was necessary because, as a prototype, the engine could not exceed 3-litres after allowance for turbocharging. The FIA's equivalency factor for two-seater cars is 1.4.

one of development that year, and the factory team acquitted itself well on its return to Le Mans in June with second place overall in the 24-Hours (Mueller/van Lennep) after a long stop to rebuild the type 915 gearbox, known to be the weakest component of the car. Martini-Porsche also picked up second place at Watkins Glen, third at Spa, sixth at the Nurburgring, and fifth at Brands Hatch. Third place in the World Championship standings was Porsche's reward, behind Matra and Gulf-Mirage.

The Porsche factory took a year off from motor racing during 1975 in preparation for the introduction of a completely new Appendix J set of regulations, due on January 1, 1976. The type 930 Turbo road car was now well established on the production line, and was to be the basis of two entirely new competition cars — the Group 4 type 934 and the Group 5 type 935. As it happened Porsche also ran the season with yet another racing car, the Group 6 type 936, with total success, to the great dismay of the much-fancied Renault team!

Leaving aside Groups 1 and 2 for saloon cars, Porsche now had a homologated Group 3 car (the Turbo 930), the Group 4 Grand Touring type 934 for the European GT and IMSA races, the

Group 5 'silhouette' machine for the World Championship for Manufacturers, and the Group 6 prototype for the World Sportscar Championship.

Taking the 934 first, it was basically the road-going 930 complete with electric windows and comfort fittings. The 2,993 cc engine, race developed and turbocharged, developed 485 horsepower in its first year, substantially more than the 330 bhp available to the Carrera RSR customers the year before. Of course the car weighed a lot more, the minimum permitted 1,120 kilogrammes, a penalty of 220 kg (485 pounds), but the cars were still very, very fast, and we gather pretty daunting around the Nurburgring. A customer could order a 934 over the counter on production of 108,000 DM, and it would be delivered ready to race with the roll-cage, extinguisher, racing seat, and all the other bits and pieces that might be needed.

Employing the standard engine casing, crank, connecting-rods, cylinder-heads and K-Jetronic injection, the major departure from standard was the inclusion of water-cooling for the air passing from the turbocharger to the induction. Twin water radiators were installed in the front air dam, and the induction air temperature was reduced from 150 degrees C to just 50 degrees, allowing the engine to run more efficiently and reliably. The water pump was driven off one of the camshafts, and the normal air-cooling fan was mounted horizontally instead of vertically.

So reliable did the 934 prove that by the end of the season the major teams had themselves raised the boost pressure, and they were obtaining 580 horsepower without encountering any problems.

The type 935 also retained the standard crankcase and crankshaft, and continued to do so even when the power output eventually exceeded 700 bhp! In 1976 form the engine was rated at 2,856 cc (92 x 70.4 mm bore and stroke) so that with the 1.4 multiplication factor applied it would have an effective overall capacity of 3,999 cc; the minimum weight for the 4-litre class was 970 kilogrammes, which the 935 met easily, needing about 70 kg of ballast, which was mainly placed at the front of the car to achieve a 47/53 per cent weight ratio.

Initially a bulky air-to-air inter-cooler was adopted, this being much lighter than the water cooler used on the 934, but midway through the first season Porsche received an FIA directive that the shape of the engine cover was not legal, so in a great hurry the

Overheating was a major problem on the turbocharged engine, before inter-coolers were fitted. Turning the air-cooling fan to the horizontal position, as on the pure racing engines, helped matters by giving a more even distribution of air over six cylinders. Originally developing 450 bhp, the engine was producing over 500 horsepower by the end of the 1974 season.

Weissach engineers had to switch to the 934's water inter-cooler system, which led to a bout of temporary unreliability. Whatever, initially the 935's full race engine developed 590 horsepower, and this was to prove sufficient.

Mention should be made of the 936, which re-adopted the stock-block 2,142 cc engine, developing 520 horspower. It is part of the 911's history to record that the 936 won every race in the 1976 World Sportscar Championship, time and again vanquishing the Renault turbo team, and carried off victories at Le Mans in 1976 and again in 1977. In 1978 the engine was substantially changed to feature water-cooled cylinder-heads, enabling Porsche's designers to fit four-valve cylinder-heads for the first time and raise the output to 580 horsepower. The Porsche team was narrowly beaten by Renault after suffering fifth-gear pinion failures on the two more powerful works cars. Returning to the Sarthe in 1979 the Porsche team again suffered defeat through unreliability, but this time they yielded in better

Still close in appearance to the road-going car, the 934 prepared for the 1976 racing season had a turbocharged 3-litre engine developing some 500 horsepower. The cooling fan was horizontal, but K-Jetronic injection was retained. In Porsche terminology, the figure 3 denotes the turbocharged engine series and the figure 4 denotes the homologation group.

Water was employed for the first time in a Porsche to cool the induction air downstream of the turbocharger. Small water radiators are located each side of the oil cooler, all incorporated in the front air dam.

Curiously devoid of advertising, this private 935 is a typical example of the series. The factory chose the 2.8-litre capacity to keep the turbocharged model within the 4-litre capacity class.

Martini-Porsche campaigned both the 935 and 936 throughout the 1976 season. In the early events the upper part of the 935, including the headlamps, remained recognizable. Power output was in the region of 650 horsepower.

By the time the 935 appeared at Mugello, advantage had been taken of the 'silhouette formula' rules to incorporate the headlamps into the area of the air dam, thus making the car faster in a straight line.

circumstances to customer-owned 935 models.

The 1976 season was a patchy one for the 935, with works drivers Jacky Ickx/Jochen Mass winning the first two rounds comfortably at Mugello and Vallelunga. However, Ickx burned out the car's clutch on the startline at Silverstone, handing victory to BMW, and before the 935 reappeared at the Nurburgring, three weeks later, the engineers had worked night and day to convert the inter-cooler in compliance with the FIA's dictate, and this led to unreliability. BMW victories at the 'Ring and in Austria brought the Munich company to within four points of Porsche's total (78 to 82), but just as Porsche began to sweat a little they found the reliability they'd been looking for, to end the season with victories at Watkins Glen and Dijon.

Porsche wasn't challenged so hotly again in the years that followed, and World Championship victories became almost totally predictable. In 1977 the factory car's power output was increased to 630 bhp, mainly as a result of fitting twin turbochargers. Throughout the season Porsches took first and second places in every qualifying round, and were only twice displaced from third place, making the result of the series a foregone conclusion.

One interesting diversion in Porsche's programme was the preparation of a 2-litre 935 for the lower division of the German GT Championship. No ordinary car was this model, dubbed the 'Baby' Porsche, because the engine was turbocharged and rated nominally at 1,425 cc to scrape into the 2-litre class. Weight was drastically pruned to bring the car close to the 735 kg minimum (it actually achieved 750 kg) and with 370 horsepower available it looked to be a runaway success. The 'Baby' only ran twice. First time out, at the Norisring, it was having teething troubles, and Jacky Ickx had to retire from the race as the car was too hot to drive — every vestige of soundproofing and insulation had been removed. Second time out, at the Hockenheim in a race preceding the German Grand Prix, Ickx started from pole position and almost lapped the field before the end. Having proved their point,

The very workmanlike interior of the Martini-Porsche 935/76 as prepared for Le Mans with a two-way radio set fitted. Fresh-air ventilation for the driver is well catered for!

Still basically the same engine as in the road-going Turbo, the 935/76 was extensively revised with such modifications as titanium conrods, a horizontal fan and an inter-cooler; it produced some 650 horsepower.

Porsche put the car away and resisted all offers to sell it.

By the end of 1977 Porsche could see that there was no real opposition in World Championship racing, and they decided to concentrate on Le Mans in order to clear the field for customer victories (the leading customers, Kremer and Georg Loos, had twin-turbo engines by now). But still the factory had one more arrow in its sling, the development of water-cooled cylinder-heads to derive even more power from the amazing six-cylinder engine.

Throughout their history Porsche had run purely air-cooled engines, as on the road cars. The 908 and 917 had been air-cooled, too, but when the FIA changed the formula to outlaw the 917 in 1972 Porsche had toyed with the idea of extracting more

Much more standard than the 935 motor in most respects, the 934 unit featured water-cooling for the turbocharged air from 150 to approximately 50 degrees C, thereby greatly increasing efficiency. Power output was in the region of 500 bhp.

power from the eight-cylinder 908 engine by fitting four-valve cylinder-heads, which were standard equipment for any other self-respecting engine builder. As air-cooled engines necessarily fit larger valves, the only way to get the smaller valves into the available space was to water-cool the heads, and an experimental engine was built in 1971. Maybe it would have been used, too, and the course of Porsche's competitions history would have been different in the 1970s, but the FIA also brought in a minimum weight limit of 650 kg for the 3-litre prototypes from 1972 onwards, and this didn't interest Porsche, who could, indeed had, built many cars substantially lighter. Clearly, the 3-litre formula would turn into a power race, and that was not interesting enough.

But water-cooling for the heads still held interest, and Porsche developed a car for 1978 which was officially known as the 935/78, though to the world at large it was simply 'Moby Dick'. Resembling a whale, and luridly painted with sponsor Martini's colours superimposed on Porsche's white livery, the 935/78 moved up a class with a nominal capacity of 3,213 cc (95.3 x 74.4 mm bore and stroke) and a rated capacity of 4,498 cc. In this

Very much an 11th-hour decision, Porsche decided during the winter of 1975/76 to take part in the World Sportscar Championship to the new Appendix J. Secret trials were conducted at the Paul Ricard circuit with the 936 painted matt black (to attract as little attention as possible) and it made its race debut at the Nurburgring in April. Rolf Stommelen was slowed with a stretched throttle cable and finished only fifth, but the 936 was not defeated again during the 1976 season despite a full-scale onslaught from Renault-Alpine, the favourites.

All subsequent rounds of the 1976 European Sportscar Championship fell to the singleton Martini-Porsche 936, usually driven by Jacky Ickx and Jochen Mass — Ickx is pictured here winning at Imola. The Renault team was thoroughly trounced, and had to wait until Le Mans in 1978 for sweet revenge.

The next stage in the development of the works team Group 5 car was the 935/77. Aerodynamic modifications included a longer tail and nearer-horizontal rear window. Ickx and Mass drove the car to victories at Silverstone, Brands Hatch and Watkins Glen during 1977.

Porsche's surprise weapon for the 1977 German GT Championship was a 1.4-litre turbocharged 935/2.0, dubbed 'The Baby'. Extensively lightened and producing 370 horsepower, it failed to finish first time out at the Norisring, where Ickx suffered badly from heat inside the car. Its next, and last outing was in an event supporting the German Grand Prix at the Hockenheimring, where Ickx started from pole position and had nearly lapped the field before the end.

The already lightweight 935 was further reduced in weight to near the 2-litre limit of 735 kilogrammes in 'Baby' form, using a spaceframe chassis. This could be called the ultimate 911 2.0!

Jacky Ickx put his name in the record books with a third consecutive Le Mans victory in 1977 and his fourth win in the classic event. Although his race was fraught with problems, the Renault onslaught crumbled and Ickx partnered Juergen Barth and Hurley Haywood to a memorable result in the 936.

higher class, the minimum weight of 1,030 kilogrammes was achieved easily.

The engine now developed no less than 750 horsepower, and the car made all others look completely out of date. In preparation for Le Mans Porsche entered the 935/78 for Silverstone, where Ickx and Mass romped away to a seven-lap victory. Confidence boosted, Porsche moved on to Le Mans, where the effort would be spearheaded by three 936s, two of them with similar (though smaller) water-cooled cylinder-heads. All three prototypes faltered, and the 935/78 didn't have a trouble-free run either, being dogged all night by a nasty misfire, and eventually Rolf Stommelen/Manfred Schurti finished the race down in eighth place. Sadly, the car wasn't raced again in 1979.

The factory team failed to achieve success at Le Mans in 1979, one 936 having a tyre blowout, which affected the water-cooling to one cylinder-head bank, the other having an alternator fail on

The final 935 development was the 935/78, seen here driven by Jochen Mass on his way to victory in the car's debut race at Silverstone, when Jacky Ickx shared the spoils. To increase the power output to an incredible 750 horsepower the 3.2-litre turbocharged engine was fitted with water-cooled, four-valve cylinder heads.

Pictured outside the research and development offices at Weissach, the 935/78 had new bodywork which pushed the regulations to their limit. The fender and door designs had to be changed when the CSI governing body threatened trouble, and the rear wing was also changed in design.

Last time out for the ultimate 935, type 78, was at Le Mans. A voracious thirst for fuel handicapped the car severely despite its speed, and a misfire lasting most of the night robbed it of any chance of success. After just two outings this ulta-expensive development was shelved.

A French-entered 935 rounds the Mulsanne corner on its way to 15th place in the 1979 Le Mans race, having run as high as third in the early hours. Dramatic overrun 'flame-out' from the exhaust was characteristic of Porsche turbo racers before the advent of economy-conscious Group C regulations.

the Mulsanne straight. All the other 3-litre prototype teams had their problems, too, and victory went to Erwin Kremer's 935 driven by Klaus Ludwig/Dick Whittington/Bill Whittington, the latter two brothers from America. Close behind them was another 935 driven by Rolf Stommelen, Dick Barbour and film star Paul Newman, Porsches, in fact, taking the top four places.

Porsche's competitions history with the 935 is summed up by John Teague in the contemporary *'Motoring News'* report of the race:

'But the day was surely Porsche's — despite the failure of the works cars. Of the 23 classified finishers 12 were products of Stuttgart, and nine of them 935s. Now that it has won everything in endurance racing, the Porsche 935 must surely go down in history as one of the great sportscars of all time, ranking alongside the Jaguar D-type, the Ferrari Testa Rossa, the Ford GT40 and

the Porsche 917.'

Like the 917, the Porsche 935 had a public following simply because it was the most powerful racing car of its era. Whereas the Grand Prix cars with 500 horsepower looked rather like Scalextric sets from a distance due to advanced chassis development, the powerful Porsches with nearly 700 horsepower available looked totally dramatic as they ducked and weaved through the corners, flames coming from the exhaust on overrun. As developments of the road-going car they lacked the finesse of a Formula 1 machine, having neither the wing area nor the ground effect to rival the single-seaters' sheer cornering power, but they were all the better for that so far as spectators were concerned.

Members of the public do not, unfortunately, ever get the chance to ride in these cars so they just have to imagine how it is to cover the straights at up to 180 mph, and dive into the turns at

2g cornering force; and if that doesn't convey the true picture, visualize a panic braking situation from 30 mph in a passenger car. If the brakes are finely tuned the 1g force generated will be enough to smash the passenger's face into the windscreen ... now double that force, and translate that into cornering power which strains the neck muscles six or eight times every lap of a six-hours race!

At the end of the 1977 racing season Porsche invited motor racing journalists to the Hockenheim circuit for rides in the World Championship-winning 935 and 936 racing cars alongside Jacky Ickx, Rolf Stommelen and Jochen Mass, and their impressions were penned for an eager public. I was privileged to ride alongside Stommelen in the 935 around the 'short' circuit,

which cuts out the long straights of the Grand Prix track, but substitutes a winding loop which crams seven fierce corners into less than two miles of track.

Leaving the pits was impressive enough. Accelerating up the white concrete pavement towards the track I was pressed hard back into the seat, gaining momentum probably faster than ever before ... but that was only part-throttle. As the huge rear tyres reached the black tarmac Stommelen floored the accelerator and the 935 hurled itself forward with enough force to jerk my head backwards and made me gasp involuntarily. A flick of the steering wheel took the car hard to the right for the 90-degree corner which immediately followed, and then into another right-hander on to the loop.

A further development of the Porsche 911's flat-six engine was designated the type 935/72 and produced for the Interscope team's entry in the 1980 Indianapolis race. The four-cam, 24-valve unit developed 630 bhp on methanol fuel. USAC promptly changed the rules to make the Porsche engine uncompetitive and the entry for Danny Ongais was withdrawn but the engine was then developed for endurance racing instead.

Outright victory at Le Mans in 1979 fell, for the first time in many years, to a production-based car. The Kremer Porsche 935K driven by Klaus Ludwig and Americans Don and Bill Whittington headed a Porsche sweep of the leading places in the wet event.

By now the car is travelling at well over 100 mph into a series of left and right curves. The engine isn't as loud as you'd expect, but the vibration and forces exerted are unimaginable. Serrated kerbstones marking the inside of corners send fierce tremors through the chassis, accompanied by harsh rumbling noises that could frighten the unwary. The Porsche's bucket seats and full harness safety belts aren't enough to prevent the passenger from being levered against the driver in the right-hand turns, so the left leg has to be stiffened against a bracing strut.

The second, flying lap is even more violent, with three distinct forces merging at each corner — braking, cornering and acceleration. Now a new vibration is felt in the corners, not from the kerbstones but from the back of the car. Stommelen turns his head: 'Can you feel the tyre vibration?' he shouts. 'I keep telling them about it.' This is a vertical shimmy that lasts about two or three seconds, the effect of tyre wind-up through the rear axle (the 935 has a solid locked differential).

At last, with a flamboyant slide through the last corner, Stommelen heads the Porsche into the pits. It is terribly quiet and peaceful. A mechanic opens the door and helps me out of the passenger seat, and I feel that my limbs have jellified — just like the effect of drinking champagne on an empty stomach. Like the previous 'victims', I have a silly grin on my face that tells the story. Then I think ... 'I was only the *passenger*. Stommelen would drive like that for two hours at a stretch, maybe more.' One's respect for the drivers is increased profoundly.

Pure racing cars such as the 936 are peripheral to this book since the only link is the production-based six-cylinder engine, and even then only the block and crankshaft are identical to the original. Nevertheless it was the 936 which kept Porsche's flag flying high, since a car loaned to Reinhold Joest finished second overall at Le Mans in 1980 despite a characteristic breakage in the five-speed gearbox during the 24-hour race.

It was Professor Dr Fuhrmann's policy to develop production-based cars in racing, and the 924 Carrera GTS was the chosen weapon in 1980, one of them finishing sixth in the hands of Juergen Barth and Manfred Schurti. The arrival of Peter Schutz as chief executive in January 1981 signalled a new era and work began at once on developing the 2.65-litre Indy engine (itself based on the 935/78 unit) for the 936, and at Le Mans in June two cars reappeared.

Reverting to fan-forced block cooling, the water-cooled heads and 24 valves allowed the engines to breathe better and attain a power output of 620 bhp at 8,000 rpm, considerably more than the 580 bhp achieved with the 2.1-litre capacity when similar engines were installed back in 1978. The Can-Am-type four-speed gearbox was employed, the ratios being rather widely spaced for a real racing car but, at least, completely reliable.

Two cars were entered for the French race, that of Jacky Ickx and Derek Bell winning handsomely without any hint of trouble, while the second car assigned to Jochen Mass/Hurley Haywood/Vern Schuppan suffered one problem after another, including a broken clutch and a defective fuel pump, to finish 12th.

Immediately after this success Mr Schutz gave the go-ahead for the new 956 model to comply with new Group C regulations coming into force in 1982. It was to be a full monocoque, wider and longer than any racing Porsche built before and taking full advantage of new knowledge about ground effects, the venturi downforce derived from a scientifically shaped floorpan. It was feared that the flat-six engine might not be suitable for this purpose, but wind-tunnel tests showed that if it was inclined upwards towards the rear at an angle of six degrees a satisfactory venturi effect could be obtained.

A completely new magnesium five-speed racing gearbox was designed for the car, with Porsche synchromesh on all gears to make endurance races a little easier for the drivers. The Bosch

Though virtually out of World Championship racing when Group C regulations were introduced in 1982, the long-lived 935 model continued to be developed in the States...and continued winning, too. Bruce Leven's ultimate 935 is illustrated at the 1984 Daytona 24-hours, where it finished fourth.

Porsche's answer to the Group C regulations under which the World Endurance Championship was to be run from 1982 was the 956, the company's first monocoque construction, ground effects competition car. At the heart of this pure racing machine is still the basic 911 engine design.

mechanical injection system had to be tuned very carefully in order to reduce the fuel consumption to an average of 55 litres per 100 kilometres in order to meet safely the new regulations.

Just as happened in 1976, Porsche met little opposition to test the 956 model thoroughly. Lancia fought valiantly in 1982 with their lighter Group 6 open cars, which were still allowed to compete, but were ineligible for points. First time out, at Silverstone, Lancia recorded an outright win, but by finishing in second place, Ickx and Bell claimed the Group C victory and maximum points. A month later at Le Mans, the three Rothmans-Porsches scored a crushing victory, cruising home in the top three places with Ickx and Bell in the lead, while John Fitzpatrick and

David Hobbs took a well-earned fourth place in their IMSA-category 935.

In a thrilling finale to the season Ickx and Bell defeated Patrese's Lancia by a mere four seconds at Brands Hatch, enabling the Belgian to claim the World Endurance Championship for Drivers. For the following season Porsche sold a dozen customer cars to private entrants, and developed the works cars with sophisticated Bosch Motronic injection/ignition systems, which showed further fuel savings. Although Lancia responded to the challenge with Group C LC2 models, powered by highly tuned Ferrari-based V8 engines, they were not able to beat the Porsches throughout the 1983 and 1984 seasons, and two

further Le Mans victories were recorded by the Stuttgart manufacturer.

The American IMSA organization had rules which differed from the FISA World Championship regulations, and to bridge the gap Porsche prepared a special version of the 956 which had the type-number 962. Specifically, the front wheels were set 12 cm further forward in the chassis in order to accommodate the pedals behind the centreline of the front wheels, this also entailing slightly different bodywork. The Americans stipulated that racing engines in the GTP category could only have two valves per cylinder and a single turbocharger, so the power unit

for IMSA was virtually the 1976 version of the 935 fully air-cooled engine, rated at 650 bhp from 2.8 litres.

The 962 made its debut at the Daytona 24-hour race in February 1984 in the hands of Mario and Mike Andretti. Mario put the car at the head of the 88-car grid in practice and led at times, but a transmission problem became evident during the evening and the car retired. Later on, in the hands of Al Holbert and Derek Bell, the Lowenbrau-sponsored 962 was able to win five races, the power unit being swapped for a 3.2-litre developing 680 bhp in order to keep up with the exceedingly fast March-Buicks. After a close tussle Randy Lanier's March took the series

For American racing, IMSA regulations depart in several respects from FISA's World Championship rules, so Porsche had to develop the 962 chassis which differed, essentially, in having the front wheels set 12 cms further forward so that the pedals lay behind the wheel centres. It also used the type 935 air-cooled, single turbo engine which necessitated a new tail cover. Mario and Mike Andretti gave the 962 its debut at Daytona in 1984, but retired due to a gearbox failure.

title, but the 962 was sure to be a leading contender in 1985.

Although the 935 model was swept away by the Group C regulations governing the World Endurance Championship, it continued to give good account of itself in America. The Daytona 24-Hours fell to the 935 seven times in succession between 1977 and 1983, and the run was broken in 1984 by the Kreepy Krauly March 83G . . . powered by a Porsche 935 engine! Throughout that seven-year period the 935 was a thoroughly consistent winner, Peter Gregg being the foremost driver until 1980, when John Fitzpatrick took over the mantle, and other prominent

winners in the next three seasons included John Paul Senior and Junior, Danny Ongais, Derek Bell, Brian Redman, Rolf Stommelen, Bob Garretson, Bob Akin, Preston Henn and Bob Wollek.

They were certainly golden years for the Porsche customers, wealthy rather than well-sponsored in the main, and able to hire top European drivers to do the hard work. Gradually, though, the GTP (prototype) category grew stronger and the 935s were made obsolete by the arrival of the Marches, the Jaguars, and renewed interest from Ford and General Motors.

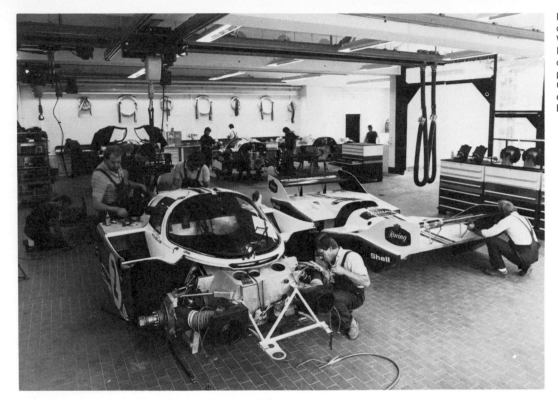

In 1984 Peter Falk's competitions department moved into a new centre at Weissach, alongside Porsche's test track. Racing cars are built there, and the department looks after the works team's preparation, but it was the World Championship winning TAG Formula 1 engines which finally forced the move into better surroundings.

In terms of victories gained, the 935 must be Porsche's most successful competition car ever, with 42 World Championship wins to its credit. Add to that some 70 IMSA victories, virtually a whitewash, and you can see that even the wonderful Porsche 917 design is rather put in the shade with a mere 29 victories, 15 scored in World Championship events and 14 in Can-Am!

CHAPTER 10

Buying a used 911

The choice, the inspection and the cost

With prices of new Porsche 911 Carreras starting at around £25,000 on the British market, possession is obviously open to wealthier people (or, more likely, those with a prospering company to foot the bill). It is now, though, that Porsche's policy of galvanizing cars properly in the mid-1970s is beginning to pay off, for even a 10-year-old example can be found in near pristine condition, and can give just as much pleasure as a brand-new 911. It may not be quite as quick, nor as economical on fuel, but all the sporting characteristics are there in abundance.

The galvanized bodies and chassis do not guarantee complete immunity to rusting. The original warranty was for six years, later extended to seven, and has been completely justified. But any process known at present has a 'life', and galvanization merely delays the onset of rusting. So even those with expired warranties may show slight signs of corrosion around the seams of the front wings, the door shuts and perhaps on the luggage compartment covers. If present at all, though, it is likely to be of a fairly minor nature and can easily be dealt with by a good bodywork specialist. Any post-1975 911 displaying serious weaknesses or corrosion will have been sadly neglected, and possibly damaged at some stage and repaired at a back-street shop, so the *caveat emptor* warning should be heeded. There *are* bad ones around, so don't get caught! As an example of how Porsches hold their value, even a 10-year-old 911 SC 2.7 can be worth as much as £8,000 and we have taken that as our base-line for parts prices at the end of this chapter.

A golden rule in buying any used Porsche over, say, five years of age is to keep £1,000 in reserve for tidying up and replacing any defective parts. Even if the body/chassis passes out alright, it is quite possible that the oil tank and the heat exchanger exhaust system will need replacing, and these two items alone can run off with £800 or so. If the vendor says these items have been attended to, ask for the receipts. Genuine factory replacement parts will be made of stainless steel and should have a life of seven or eight years, but passable replicas made of mild steel are available costing around half the price, but lasting half as long — pay your money and take your choice.

Porsches fall roughly into three categories — the rust age up to 1969, the interim stage up to 1974, and the galvanized age from 1975 onwards. Until 1969 Porsche's rust protection was as good as any rival's, but that wasn't particularly good, and we must remember that we are now talking about cars which are 16 years old, so by normal standards they are due for scrapping. Clearly some earlier 911s will have been looked after well, may have had some extra underbody protection, or may have been renovated expertly, so these would be well worth inspecting.

Outward visual checks should include the outer sills, jacking points, lamp surrounds, the backs of light units, and the front apron. It is most important then to get the car on to a hoist to inspect the floor pan, the torsion-bar mounting points, the inner sills and the brake lines, and to look for oil or hydraulic leaks. Most Porsche dealers would be happy to inspect the car and make out a detailed report for around £75, or failing that the AA operates a used-car inspection service. This is strongly recommended for a comparatively expensive car like a Porsche, which could be worth as much as £5,000 at 15 years, or could just as easily be worthless.

The original O-series cars with Solex carburettors (up to

February 1966) would be prone to nasty flat spots, which could spoil the driving pleasure, but the Weber-equipped cars from that date to the advent of Bosch injection are much nicer to drive, and more powerful. All should be capable of achieving 125 mph or more, but there were reservations about the handling — strong understeer could turn into sharp oversteer.

The introduction of the longer wheelbase on the B-series, from August 1968 to July 1969, brought about great improvements in handling, especially on the fuel-injected 'E' and 'S' versions with their six-inch rims. Any 'S' could be considered a collector's item

A classic of its time, and a shape which will always be associated with a special type of motoring.

today if in nice condition, and the thump in the back accompanied by a purposeful engine and exhaust note marks out this model as an enthusiast's car. They were, however, rather prone to oiling their plugs in traffic. Although Targas were not imported to Britain until 1973 some did find their way into the country, and particular attention should be paid to the body condition because some of the panels are stressed, making repair a little more difficult.

Starting with the C-series 2.2-litre models in the autumn of 1969, Porsche began to pay more attention to rust-proofing by applying the Tectyl process to the underside and sills. Although any oil-based process applied after manufacture will inevitably dry out eventually, its early application will have delayed the onset of oxidation. The 2.2-litre models were rather more flexible than the previous versions and would be more relaxing to drive.

From May 1971, four months before the advent of the 2.4-litre E-series, the sills were made of galvanized steel. Later on the fully galvanized cars (from January 1975) were given the six-year Longlife warranty against rust holes, so it can be assumed that six years is the *minimum* life for galvanized parts. Cars made during the early-70's are still prone to showing rust bubbles around the headlamps and front aprons, but they stand a good chance of being sound structurally.

The E-series can be identified by the oil filler cover in the right-hand body panel, behind the driver's door, but the F-series, starting August 1973, put the oil tank back in its proper place in the engine compartment. The entire floor pan of the F-series was galvanized and Tectyl-treated, though the sought-after 1973 Carrera did not have this treatment as it added weight. Normally the Carreras have been well looked after because of their rarity value, but look out for water-sealing problems in the area of the Glaverbel windscreen which, being thinner and lighter than standard, did not always seal properly.

From 1975 onwards, as stated, the entire bodyshells were fully galvanized and given a six-year warranty against rust holes (but not against surface oxidation or paint bubbles), so mechanical condition is the main concern. The same basic principles apply to Porsches as any other cars — checking for exhaust smoke after the car has been idling for a couple of minutes (wear in the valve guides), untoward engine noises, clutch play — especially important with the Sportomatic — examination of heat exchangers and for oil tank seepage. Stainless-steel components were fitted from 1975 onwards, but these are frighteningly expensive if the buyer is not prepared for a large outlay. A neglected heat exchanger (the baffle that surrounds the exhaust manifold) will allow fumes to enter the car, which could have fatal consequences, so do *not* try to save money on that score!

To check the condition of a Sportomatic transmission, drive the car and make sure that the solenoid-operated clutch is engaging and disengaging properly without any time lag. To check the clutch, hold the car on the footbrake and press the accelerator with the gear lever in Drive. The torque converter should allow the revs to rise to 2,800 rpm then hold steady; if there is any wear, or oil, on the plates, the revs will increase after two or three seconds. Do not run this test any longer than five or six seconds as the torque converter will start over-heating. The Sportomatic semi-automatic transmission went out of production in May 1979.

The nice thing about Porsches is that they get better every year, and sometimes technical changes are even made midway through a model year. One little component that has always been troublesome since the beginning is the hydraulic timing-chain tensioner, a spring blade which, sooner or later in the car's life, will fail. It is not a bad idea to replace this spring every four or five years as preventive maintenance, because its breakage can result in slipped timing and an expensive engine repair. Should the engine suddenly begin to make a terrible rattle, switch off immediately and resort to public transport. Equally important is the retaining nut on the camshaft sprocket, which will cause extensive damage in the valve department if it works loose.

Pretty well any job on a Porsche engine means taking the power unit out of the car, which is easy for a well equipped workshop, but considerably more difficult for a home handyman. As special tools are needed for most jobs, engine renovation and repairs will be beyond most owners anyway. London rates will be over £20 an hour, so it is always advisable (a) to go to a Porsche dealer or specialist, and (b) get a written estimate before the job is put in hand. Later cars, with 12,000-miles service intervals, should compare very well on running costs against other specialist makes which have to be tuned and serviced every 3,000-5,000 miles.

Certainly, for everyday use, the post-1973 G, H and I-series cars should be preferred for practical reasons — better rust-proofing, improved ventilation, better aerodynamics (the bib spoiler became standard a year before), high-back seats, energy-absorbing bumpers, and the 12,000-mile service intervals all added up to a package that combines sportiness with practicality. A production Carrera 3 (1975-77) with 200 horsepower and a distinctive 'cam' effect from 4,000 rpm, is a particularly nice car to own, but perhaps that's a purely personal choice.

In case the log book is not specific, a quick check on engine types. All the air-cooled engines have a plastic shroud ducting air from the fan to the cylinders, and until 1976 red plastic was always used for the most powerful engine in the range — the 911S and Carrera. Green shrouds were used for the 911E and black shrouds for the T. Since 1976 all models, including the Turbo, have had red shrouds.

Porsches have always been designed and built by engineers who are also enthusiasts, people who know about fast driving. Quick steering, light controls and a tremendously satisfying response are the hallmarks of the 911 series, which is full of qualities that sets it apart from the merely mundane methods of transport.

Listed below are typical 1985 prices for Porsche original parts for a 1975 911 2.7 litre model. A price guide like this will indicate the cost of replacing parts which might be suspect at the time of purchasing.

Typical 1985 UK prices (net of VAT) for new or exchange parts 1975 911 2.7-litre

Part	Part number	Price
Heat exchanger/exhaust (left or right)	930.211.025.01	£ 198.00
Oil tank	911.107.006.20	£ 210.84
Inner sill, left	911.501.123.03	£ 13.72
Outer sill, left	911.503.401.04	£ 18.52
Hydraulic tensioner conversion kit — left	930.105.911.00	£ 73.10
Engine oil cooler — exchange	911.107.041.X	£ 152.49
Front pads	911.351.938.00	£ 16.00
Rear pads	911.352.949.00	£ 20.78
Front strut insert (Boge)	911.341.913.03	£ 56.92
Front strut, left (Bilstein)	911.341.041.33	£ 166.08
Fuel pump	930.608.111.00	£ 134.19
Clutch centre plate	915.116.011.14	£ 97.60
Clutch pressure plate — exchange	915.116.001.JX	£ 58.00
Gearbox, 5-speed — exchange (915/43)	915.300.010.CX	£1,722.37
Gearbox, Sportomatic (925/02)	925.300.010.02	£2,157.57

Porsche 911 model recognition and serial numbers

O Series. Model 901, first shown at Frankfurt in September 1963, as an eventual replacement for the 356 model. Although it bore a family resemblance to the 356 it was longer, narrower, and had a longer wheelbase to allow more interior space. It had a completely new six-cylinder engine of 1,991cc with a maximum power output of 130bhp at 6,200rpm. A top speed of 130 mph was claimed. Production commenced in September 1964, initially alongside the 356 until May 1965, when the first right-hand drive 911 was manufactured for export to Britain.

February 1966 – Solex triple-choke carburettors replaced by Webers. August 1966 – First Targa models announced for production commencing Spring 1967. 911S version announced with 160bhp, forged alloy pistons, revised (901/02) camshafts, larger valves and 9.8:1 compression. New heat exchangers also fitted to 911. The 911S had thicker, ventilated disc brakes and 5J forged alloy wheels, and a leather-covered steering wheel was fitted. The maximum speed of this model is 140mph.

Year	Body	Type	Chassis numbers	Engine type	6-cylinder bore x stroke	C.R.	Power bhp/rpm	Torque lb/ft
1963	Coupe	901	–	901	80×66 (1,991cc)	9.0:1	130 @ 6,200	119 @ 4,600
1964/65	Coupe	911	300001-300235	901/01	80×66	9.0:1	130 @ 6,100	128 @ 4,200
1964/66	Coupe	911	300236-305100	901/01	80×66	9.0:1	130 @ 6,100	128 @ 4,200
1966/67	Coupe	911	305101-308552	901/05	80×66	9.0:1	130 @ 6,100	128 @ 4,200
	Targa	911	500001-500718	901/06	80×66	9.0:1	130 @ 6,100	128 @ 4,200
	Coupe	911S	305101S-308523S	901/02	80×66	9.8:1	160 @ 6,600	133 @ 5,200
	Targa	911S	500001S-500718S	901/02	80×66	9.8:1	160 @ 6,600	133 @ 5,200

A Series. In August 1967 two new versions were announced, the 911L (virtually the old 911 but with different camshafts, and still 130bhp) and the less expensive 911T with virtually 912 body specification. The 911T had cast-iron cylinders, lower compression, a simplified crankshaft, smaller valves and 110bhp. External identification is the adoption of 5½J×15 wheels, and black wiper arms parking in front of the driver. Four-speed Sportomatic transmission introduced as a 990 DM option.

Year	Body	Type	Chassis numbers	Engine type	6-cylinder bore x stroke	C.R.	Power bhp/rpm	Torque lb/ft
1967/68	Coupe	911-US	11830001-11830473	901/14	80×66 (1,991cc)	9:1	130 @ 6,100	130 @ 4,200
	*K-Coupe	911	11835001-11835742	901/06	80×66	9:1	130 @ 6,100	130 @ 4,200
	Targa	911	11880001-11880268	901/06	80×66	9:1	130 @ 6,100	130 @ 4,200
	Coupe	911L	11810001-11810720	901/06	80×66	9:1	130 @ 6,100	130 @ 4,200
	Targa	911L	11860001-11860307	901/06	80×66	9:1	130 @ 6,100	130 @ 4,200
	Coupe	911T	11820001-11820928	901/03	80×66	8.6:1	110 @ 5,800	115 @ 4,200
	K-Coupe	911T	11825001-11825683	901/03	80×66	8.6:1	110 @ 5,800	115 @ 4,200
	Targa	911T	11870001-11870521	901/03	80×66	8.6:1	110 @ 5,800	115 @ 4,200
	Coupe	911S	11800001-11801267	901/02	80×66	9.8:1	160 @ 6,600	133 @ 5,200
	Targa	911S	11850001-11850442	901/02	80×66	9.8:1	160 @ 6,600	133 @ 5,200
	Coupe	911L-US	11805001-11805449	901/14	80×66	9:1	130 @ 6,100	130 @ 4,200
	Targa	911L-US	11855001-11855134	901/14	80×66	9:1	130 @ 6,100	130 @ 4,200

*K-Coupe is Karmann body.

B Series. The wheelbase was extended by 57mm to 2,268mm (89.3 inches), and the wheelarches flared to accommodate 6J×15 wheels now offered on the 911E and 911S versions. Starting August 1968, the B-Series also introduced Bosch mechanical fuel injection,which helped to increase the power of the E and S by 10bhp. Magnesium crankcase introduced to T, E and S. Twin batteries fitted, and generator increased to 770W, quartz halogen main beams became standard, and heated rear windows fitted. Self-levelling gas front struts fitted as standard on the 911E and optionally on the 911T. See text for further details. External identifications – raised door handle protecting push-button release, padded spokes on steering wheel, and Targa version with air extractor vents in roll-over hoop.

Year	Body	Type	Chassis numbers	Engine type	6-cylinder bore x stroke	C.R.	Power bhp/rpm	Torque lb/ft
1968/69	Coupe	911T	119000001-119000343	901/03 or 13	80×66 (1,991cc)	8.6:1	110 @ 5,800	115 @ 4,200
	K-Coupe	911T	119120001-119123561	901/16 or 19	80×66	8.6:1	110 @ 5,800	115 @ 4,200
	Targa	911T	119100001-119111282	901/19	80×66	8.6:1	110 @ 5,800	115 @ 4,200
	Coupe	911E	119200001-119200954	901/09 or 11	80×66	9.1:1	140 @ 6,500	130 @ 4,500
	K-Coupe	911E	119220001-119221014	901/09 or 11	80×66	9.1:1	140 @ 6,500	130 @ 4,500
	Targa	911E	119210001-119210858	901/09 or 11	80×66	9.1:1	140 @ 6,500	130 @ 4,500
	Coupe	911S	119300001-119301492	901/10	80×66	9.9:1	170 @ 6,800	135 @ 5,500
	Targa	911S	119310001-119310614	901/10	80×66	9.9:1	170 @ 6,800	135 @ 5,500

C and D Series. These two virtually identical series for the 1970 and 1971 model years (from September 1969 to August 1971) featured the bored-out 2.2-litre engines which provided more power and torque. Clutch diameters were increased to 225mm on the E and S injection models. Four-wheel ventilated disc brakes were introduced to the T version.

Year	Body	Type	Chassis numbers	Engine type	6-cylinder bore x stroke	C.R.	Power bhp/rpm	Torque lb/ft
1969/70	Coupe	911T	9110100001-9110102418	911/03	84×66 (2,195cc)	8.6:1	125 @ 5,800	131 @ 4,200
	K-Coupe	911T	9110120001-9110124126	911/07	84×66	8.6:1	125 @ 5,800	131 @ 4,200
	Targa	911T	9110110001-9110112545	911/06	84×66	8.6:1	125 @ 5,800	131 @ 4,200
	Coupe	911E	9110200001-9110201304	911/01	84×66	9.1:1	155 @ 6,200	141 @ 4,500
	K-Coupe	911E	9110220001-9110220667	911/04	84×66	9.1:1	155 @ 6,200	141 @ 4,500
	Targa	911E	9110210001-9110210933	911/04	84×66	9.1:1	155 @ 6,200	141 @ 4,500
	Coupe	911S	9110320001-9110301744	911/02	84×66	9.8:1	180 @ 6,500	147 @ 5,200
1970/71	Coupe	911T	9111100001-9111110583	911/00	84×66	8.6:1	125 @ 5,800	131 @ 4,200
	K-Coupe	911T	9111120001-9111121934	911/07	84×66	8.6:1	125 @ 5,800	131 @ 4,200
	Targa	911T	9111110001-9111113476	911/06	84×66	8.6:1	125 @ 5,800	131 @ 4,200
	Coupe	911E	9111200001-9111201088	911/01	84×66	9.1:1	155 @ 6,200	141 @ 4,500
	Targa	911E	9111210001-9111210935	911/01	84×66	9.1:1	155 @ 6,200	141 @ 4,500
	Coupe	911S	9111300001-9111301430	911/02	84×66	9.8:1	180 @ 6,500	147 @ 5,200
	Targa	911S	9111310001-9111310788	911/02	84×66	9.8:1	180 @ 6,500	147 @ 5,200

E and F Series. An increase in engine capacity to 2,341cc by means of a longer stroke distinguished the 1971 models. At the same time compression ratios were reduced so that the cars would run on 91-octane unleaded fuel, as a way of complying with America's increasingly stringent emission laws. To meet the increased power and torque a new type 915 gearbox was adopted, and this differed in having a new change pattern with fifth and reverse gears out to the right. The E Series is distinguished by having the oil tank moved forwards, and the filler behind the right-hand door.

For the 1972 model year, the F Series moved the oil tank back to its normal position in the right-hand rear wing. At the same time the tank was increased in capacity, so that the service intervals could be extended to 12,000 miles, and was made of stainless steel for longer life. The silencer was also made of stainless steel. The 911E had new ATS pressure-cast wheels, optional for the 911T. The front air dam, standard on the 911S the previous year, became standard equipment for all versions.

Year	Body	Type	Chassis numbers	Engine type	6-cylinder bore x stroke	C.R.	Power bhp/rpm	Torque lb/ft
1971/72	Coupe	911T	9112500001-9112501963	911/57	84×70.4 (2,341cc)	7.5:1	130 @ 5,600	145 @ 4,000
	Targa	911T	9112510001-9112511523	911/57	84×70.4	7.5:1	130 @ 5,600	145 @ 4,000
	Coupe	911E	9112200001-9112201124	911/52	84×70.4	8.0:1	165 @ 6,200	152 @ 4,500
	Targa	911E	9112210001-9112210861	911/52	84×70.4	8.0:1	165 @ 6,200	152 @ 4,500
	Coupe	911S	9112300001-9112301750	911/53	84×70.4	8.5:1	190 @ 6,500	159 @ 5,200
	Targa	911S	9112310001-9112310989	911/53	84×70.4	8.5:1	190 @ 6,500	159 @ 5,200
	Coupe	911T-US	9112100001-9112102931	911/51	84×70.4	7.5:1	140 @ 5,600	145 @ 4,000
	Targa	911T-US	9112110001-9112111821	911/51	84×70.4	7.5:1	140 @ 5,600	145 @ 4,000
1972/73	Coupe	911T	9113500001-9113501875	911/57	84×70.4	7.5:1	130 @ 5,600	145 @ 4,000
	Targa	911T	9113510001-9113511541	911/57	84×70.4	7.5:1	130 @ 5,600	145 @ 4,000
	Coupe	911E	9113200001-9113201366	911/52	84×70.4	8.0:1	165 @ 6,200	152 @ 4,500
	Targa	911E	9113210001-9113211055	911/52	84×70.4	8.0:1	165 @ 6,200	152 @ 4,500
	Coupe	911S	9113300001-9113301430	911/53	84×70.4	8.5:1	190 @ 6,500	159 @ 5,200
	Targa	911S	9113310001-9113310925	911/53	84×70.4	8.5:1	190 @ 6,500	159 @ 5,200
	Coupe	Carrera	9113600001-9113601036	911/83	90×70.4 (2,687cc)	8.5:1	210 @ 6,300	188 @ 5,100
	Coupe	911T-US	9113100001-9113101252	911/51	84×70.4	7.5:1	140 @ 5,600	145 @ 4,000
	Targa	911T-US	9113110001-9113110781	911/51	84×70.4	7.5:1	140 @ 5,600	145 @ 4,000

G and H Series. Following the pilot series of the Carrera model at 2.7 litres, primarily intended for competitions work, the G Series 911 range followed suit with a similar 2,687cc engine, but with Bosch K-Jetronic injection. The T and E versions were discontinued, so the range consisted of the 911, the 911S and the Carrera, the latter having mechanical injection. New, collapsible bumper bars were featured on the 1974 models, doing away with the distinctive horn grilles on each side of the luggage compartment lid, and new seats with built-in headrests became part of the equipment.

Year	Body	Type	Chassis numbers	Engine type	6-cylinder bore x stroke	C.R.	Power bhp/rpm	Torque lb/ft
1973/74	Coupe	911	9114100001-9114104014	911/92	90×70.4 (2,687cc)	8.0:1	150 @ 5,700	174 @ 3,800
	Targa	911	9114110001-9114113110	911/92	90×70.4	8.0:1	150 @ 5,700	174 @ 3,800
	Coupe	911S	9114300001-9114301359	911/93	90×70.4	8.5:1	175 @ 5,800	174 @ 4,000
	Targa	911S	9114310001-9114310898	911/93	90×70.4	8.5:1	175 @ 5,800	174 @ 4,000
	Coupe	Carrera-US	9114400001-9114400528	911/93	90×70.4	8.5:1	175 @ 5,800	174 @ 4,000
	Coupe	Carrera	9114600001-9114601036	911/83	90×70.4	8.5:1	210 @ 6,300	188 @ 5,100
	Targa	Carrera	9114610001-9114610433	911/83	90×70.4	8.5:1	210 @ 6,300	188 @ 5,100

Year	Body	Type	Chassis numbers	Engine type	6-cylinder bore x stroke	C.R.	Power bhp/rpm	Torque lb/ft
1974/75	Coupe	911	9115100001-9115101238	911/41	90×70.4	8.0:1	150 @ 5,700	174 @ 3,800
	Targa	911	9115110001-9115110998	911/41	90×70.4	8.0:1	150 @ 5,700	174 @ 3,800
	Coupe	911S	9115300001-9115300385	911/42	90×70.4	8.5:1	175 @ 5,800	174 @ 4,000
	Coupe	911S-US	9115200001-9115202310	911/43	90×70.4	8.5:1	165 @ 5,800	166 @ 4,000
	Targa	911S	9115310001-9115310266	911/42	90×70.4	8.5:1	175 @ 5,800	174 @ 4,000
	Targa	911S-US	9115210001-9115211517	911/43	90×70.4	8.5:1	165 @ 5,800	166 @ 4,000
	Coupe	Carrera	9115600001-9115600518	911/83	90×70.4	8.5:1	210 @ 6,300	188 @ 5,100
	Coupe	Carrera-US	9115400001-9115400395	911/43	90×70.4	8.5:1	165 @ 5,800	166 @ 4,000
	Targa	Carrera	9115610001-9115610197	911/83	90×70.4	8.5:1	210 @ 6,300	188 @ 5,100
	Coupe	930	9305700001-9305700284	930/50	95×70.4 (2,994cc)	6.5:1	260 @ 5,500	253 @ 4,000

I and J Series. With the 930 Turbo successfully launched (on what was supposed to be a limited production run for homologation purposes), the Carrera 3 was announced during 1975 for the 1976 model year, using the same die-cast aluminium crankcase. Bosch K-Jetronic injection replaced mechanical injection, and despite the extra capacity the power dropped to 200bhp, though with greatly improved torque. The range was now simplified with the luxury-equipped 911 2.7, the Carrera 3 and the Turbo models.

Year	Body	Type	Chassis numbers	Engine type	6-cylinder bore x stroke	C.R.	Power bhp/rpm	Torque lb/ft
1975/76	Coupe	911	9116300001-9116301868	911/81	90×70.4 (2,687cc)	8.5:1	165 @ 5,800	174 @ 4,000
	Coupe	911S-US	9116200001-9116202079	911/82	90×70.4	8.5:1	165 @ 5,800	174 @ 4,000
	Targa	911	9116310001-9116311576	911/81	90×70.4	8.5:1	165 @ 5,800	174 @ 4,000
	Targa	911S-US	9116210001-9116212175	911/84	90×70.4	8.5:1	165 @ 5,800	174 @ 4,000
	Coupe	Carrera 3	9116600001-9116601093	930/02	95×70.4 (2,994cc)	8.5:1	200 @ 6,000	188 @ 4,200
	Targa	Carrera 3	9116610001-9116610479	930/02	95×70.4	8.5:1	200 @ 6,000	188 @ 4,200
	Coupe	930	9306700001-9306700157	930/50	95×70.4	6.5:1	260 @ 5,500	253 @ 4,000
	Coupe	930-US	9306800001-9306800530	930/51	95×70.4	6.5:1	245 @ 5,500	253 @ 4,000
1976/77	Targa	911	9117300001-9117302449	911/81	90×70.4	8.5:1	165 @ 5,800	174 @ 4,000
	Coupe	911S-US	9117200001-9117203388	911/85	90×70.4	8.5:1	165 @ 5,800	174 @ 4,000
	Targa	911	9117310001-9117311724	911/81	90×70.4	8.5:1	165 @ 5,800	174 @ 4,000
	Targa	911S-US	9117210001-9117212747	911/85	90×70.4	8.5:1	165 @ 5,800	174 @ 4,000
	Coupe	Carrera	9117600001-9117601473	930/02	95×70.4	8.5:1	200 @ 6,000	188 @ 4,200
	Targa	Carrera 3	9117610001-9117610646	930/02	95×70.4	8.5:1	200 @ 6,000	188 @ 4,200
	Coupe	930	9307700001-9307700695	930/52	95×70.4	6.5:1	260 @ 5,500	253 @ 4,000
	Coupe	930-US	9307800001-9307800727	930/54	95×70.4	6.5:1	245 @ 5,500	253 @ 4,000

K and L Series. One more major revision for the 911 family, with the 911 becoming the 911 SC with virtually the Carrera 3 engine, though with new camshafts, an air pump for all markets, and an output of 180 horsepower. The Carrera's body shell with flared arches was retained for the 911 SC, and the wider wheels were fitted. The engine, with a stronger crankshaft and larger bearings, had more torque than that of the Carrera version. The five-speed gearbox became standard for all markets. The Turbo was increased in capacity to 3.3 litres by means of enlarging the bore and stroke, power rising to 300bhp. An air-to-air inter-cooler was fitted as standard. Brake servos became standard for all models, and a new Porsche-designed clutch disc hub eliminated gear chatter. The engine in the Turbo 3.3 was moved back 30mm as a result. The Turbo now had the full type 917 brake system, with four piston calipers and cross-drilled discs.

Year	Body	Type	Chassis numbers	Engine type	6-cylinder bore x stroke	C.R.	Power bhp/rpm	Torque lb/ft
1977/78	Coupe	911SC	9118300001-9118302438	930/03	95×70.4 (2,994cc)	8.5:1	180 @ 5,500	188 @ 4,200
	Coupe	911SC-US	9118200001-9118202436	930/04/06	95×70.4	8.5:1	180 @ 5,500	175 @ 4,200
	Targa	911SC	9118310001-9118311729	930/03	95×70.4	8.5:1	180 @ 5,500	188 @ 4,200
	Targa	911SC-US	9118210001-9118212579	930/04/06	95×70.4	8.5:1	180 @ 5,500	175 @ 4,200
	Coupe	930	9308700001-9308700735	930/60	97×74.4 (3,299cc)	7.0:1	300 @ 5,500	304 @ 4,000
	Coupe	930-US	9308800001-9308800461	930/61/63	97×74.4	7.0:1	265 @ 5,500	290 @ 4,000
1978/79	Coupe	911SC	9119300001-9119303318	930/03	95×70.4	8.5:1	180 @ 5,500	188 @ 4,200
	Coupe	911SC-US	9119200001-9119202013	930/04/06	95×70.4	8.5:1	180 @ 5,500	175 @ 4,200
	Targa	911SC	9119310001-9119311874	930/03	95×70.4	8.5:1	180 @ 5,500	188 @ 4,200
	Targa	911SC-US	9119210001-9119211965	930/04/06.	95×70.4	8.5:1	180 @ 5,500	175 @ 4,200
	Coupe	930	9309700001-9309700820	930/60	97×74.4	7.0:1	300 @ 5,500	304 @ 4,000
	Coupe	930-US	9309800001-9309800781	930/61/63	97×74.4	7.0:1	265 @ 5,500	290 @ 4,000

A Series. The model reference has gone back to 'A' denoted in the chassis number by 91A0, and in future years will be incorporated in the middle of the chassis number, the letters BS, CS etcetera preceding the numbers. The 1980 model 911SC received 'optimized' engine settings with tighter tolerances and revised ignition timing, and this revision served to increase the power to 188bhp and at the same time improve petrol economy by 10 per cent (the main improvement being in the urban cycle). A new type of oil cooler was fitted on the 911 and the Turbo, and the 911 SC also took on a better appearance with matching cloth upholstery for the rear seats, instead of vinyl covering.

Year	Body	Type	Chassis number	Engine type	6-cylinder bore x stroke	C.R.	Power bhp/rpm	Torque lb/ft
1979/80	*Coupe/ Targa	911SC	91AO130001-91AO134831	930/09	95×70.4 (2,994cc)	8.6:1	188 @ 5,500	195 @ 4,300
	Coupe	911SC-US	91AO140001-91AO144272	930/07	95×70.4	9.3:1	180 @ 5,500	180 @ 4,200
	Coupe	930	93AO070001-93AO070840	930/60	97×74.4 (3,299cc)	7.0:1	300 @ 5,500	303 @ 4,000

*In this model year only, there was no distinction in chassis numbers between coupe and Targa bodies.

B Series. Major improvements in power and fuel economy were featured on the 1981 model year 911 SC. The compression ratio was increased from 8.6 to 9.8:1 with new pistons and further optimization of the ignition and K-Jetronic settings, increasing the power from 188bhp at 5,900rpm to 204bhp at the same engine speed; the torque value remained unchanged. The maximum speed rose to 146mph and 0.75 sec was pared from the 0-60mph acceleration time. The engine now required 98ROZ (4-star in the UK) fuel, but a 21 per cent improvement in overall fuel economy was found. In the urban cycle, for instance, the consumption improved from 16.33 to 21.08mpg. The only visual change on the B Series model was the inclusion of turn indicator repeaters on the sides of the front wings. No changes were made to the specification of the Turbo.

Year	Body	Type	Chassis number	Engine type	6-cylinder bore x stroke	C.R.	Power bhp/rpm	Torque lb/ft
1980/81	Coupe	911SC	WPO22291ZBS100001- WPO22291ZBS103181	930/10	95×70.4 (2,994cc)	9.8:1	204 @ 5,900	195 @ 4,300
	Targa	911SC	WPO22291ZBS140001- WPO22291ZBS141703	930/10	95×70.4	9.8:1	204 @ 5,900	195 @ 4,300
	Coupe	911SC-US	WPOAAO91BS120001- WPOAAO91BS121573	930/16	95×70.4	9.3:1	180 @ 5,500	180 @ 4,200
	Targa	911SC-US	WPOEAO91BS160001- WPOEAO91BS161407	930/16	95×70.4	9.3:1	180 @ 5,500	180 @ 4,200
	Coupe	911SC-Japan	WPO22291ZBS129500- WPO22291ZBS129622	930/17	95×70.4	9.3:1	180 @ 5,500	180 @ 4,200
	Targa	911SC-Japan	WPO22291ZBS169500- WPO22291ZBS169510	930/17	95×70.4	9.3:1	180 @ 5,500	180 @ 4,200
	Coupe	930	WPO22293ZBS000001- WPO22293ZBS000698	930/60	97×74.4 (3,299cc)	7.0:1	300 @ 5,500	303 @ 4,000
	Coupe	930-Canada	WPOJAO93BS050001- WPOJAO93BS050063	930/60	97×74.4	7.0:1	300 @ 5,500	303 @ 4,000

C Series. Only minor changes were made in the 1982 model year. The alternators on the 911 SC and Turbo models were uprated from 980 to 1,050 Watts and had an integral regulator. On the 911 SC, headlamp washers became standard equipment, the transmission differential gears were strengthened, and new graduations were seen on the oil temperature gauge. The wheels had black centres and polished rims. As optional equipment, the 911 SC could be ordered with a deeper air dam and a larger rear wing, similar in appearance to the Turbo's fittings, in order to increase the aerodynamic downforce.

Year	Body	Type	Chassis number	Engine type	6-cylinder bore x stroke	C.R.	Power bhp/rpm	Torque lb/ft
1981/82	Coupe	911SC	WPO22291ZCS100001- WPO22291ZCS103307	930/10	95×70.4 (2,994cc)	9.8:1	204 @ 5,900	195 @ 4,300
	Targa	911SC	WPO22291ZCS140001- WPO22291ZCS141737	930/10	95×70.4	9.8:1	204 @ 5,900	195 @ 4,300
	Coupe	911SC-US	WPOAAO91CS120001- WPOAAO91CS122457	930/16	95×70.4	9.3:1	180 @ 5,500	180 @ 4,200
	Targa	911SC-US	WPOEAO91CS160001- WPOEAO91CS162426	930/16	95×70.4	9.3:1	180 @ 5,500	180 @ 4,200
	Coupe	911SC-Japan	WPO22291ZCS109501- WPO22291ZCS109628	930/17	95×70.4	9.3:1	180 @ 5,500	180 @ 4,200
	Coupe	930	WPO22293ZCS000001- WPO22293ZCS000938	930/60	97×74.4 (3,299cc)	7.0:1	300 @ 5,500	303 @ 4,000
	Coupe	930-Canada	WPOJAO93CS05001- WPOJAO93CS050089	930/60	97×74.4	7.0:1	300 @ 5,500	303 @ 4,000

D Series. The cabriolet model first seen at the Geneva Show in March was now in production, with a fully convertible top. The Targa model's roll-over bar was deleted and the chassis was reinforced, weights remaining identical at 1,160kg. All models had a new primary silencer to help reduce noise levels and meet higher emission requirements, the red heater override control between the seats was finally deleted, and four radio speakers became standard equipment. Provision was made for the installation of fixed-length rear seat belts.

The Turbo model received a number of modifications which increased the torque value from 42 to 44mkp (303 to 318lb ft) by means of a new ignition distributor, a fuel distributor with a capsule valve to improve throttle response and a new exhaust system with twin tailpipes. Interior heating was improved with two extra blowers serving the footwell area. The Turbo's fuel consumption was substantially improved, by as much as 29 per cent in the urban cycle from 14.1 to 18.2mpg and from 18.5 to 23.9mpg at 75mph. American versions had a modified acceleration control unit and an improved oxygen sensor.

Year	Body	Type	Chassis number	Engine type	6-cylinder bore x stroke	C.R.	Power bhp/rpm	Torque lb/ft
1982/83	Coupe	911SC	WPO22291ZDS100001- WPO22291ZDS102995	930/10	95×70.4	9.8:1	204 @ 5,900	195 @ 4,300
	Targa	911SC	WPO22291ZDS140001- WPO22291ZDS141258	930/10	95×70.4	9.8:1	204 @ 5,900	195 @ 4,300
	Cabriolet	911SC	WPO22291ZDS150001- WPO22291ZDS152406	930/10	95×70.4	9.8:1	204 @ 5,500	195 @ 4,300
	Coupe	911SC-US	WPOAAO91DS120001- WPOAAO91DS122559	930/16	95×70.4	9.3:1	180 @ 5,500	180 @ 4,200
	Targa	911SC-US	WPOEAO91DS160001- WPOEAO91DS161430	930/16	95×70.4	9.3:1	180 @ 5,500	180 @ 4,200
	Cabriolet	911SC-US	WPOEAO91DS170001- WPOEAO91DS171781	930/16	95×70.4	9.3:1	180 @ 5,500	180 @ 4,200
	Coupe	911SC-Japan	WPO22291ZDS109501- WPO22291ZDS109645	930/17	95×70.4	9.3:1	180 @ 5,500	180 @ 4,200
	Targa	911SC-Japan	WPO22291ZDS149501- WPO22291ZDS149562	930/17	95×70.4	9.3:1	180 @ 5,500	180 @ 4,200
	Cabriolet	911SC-Japan	WPO22291ZDS159501- WPO22291ZDS159590	930/17	95×70.4	9.3:1	180 @ 5,500	180 @ 4,200
	Coupe	930	WPO22293ZDS000001- WPO22293ZDS001015	930/66	97×74.4	7.0:1	300 @ 5,500	318 @ 4,000
	Coupe	930-Canada	WPOJAO93DS05001- WPOJAO93DS050065	930/66	97×74.4	7.0:1	300 @ 5,500	318 @ 4,000

E Series. Introduction of the 911 Carrera model with a 3.2-litre engine and 231bhp, with still higher performance and better fuel economy. Adoption of the Turbo model's crankshaft increased the stroke to 74.4mm while the bore remained at 95 mm, giving a swept capacity of 3,164cc. Digital Motor Electronics (DME) replaced K-Jetronic (requiring a new flywheel with suitable calibrations) and the compression ratio was increased to 10.3:1. Cylinder-head gaskets were deleted, as on the Turbo, new pistons fitted, new timing chain tensioners were lubricated by the main oil system, a new exhaust system was specified, brake discs were 3.5mm thicker, a pressure-limiting device (from the 928S) installed in the brake circuit, an eight-inch brake servo fitted, fourth and fifth gear ratios were raised and the gearbox received an external cooler.

The Carrera could also be ordered with the Turbo's body and suspension (M-491) in markets other than the UK. As standard equipment the Carrera had pierced alloy wheels similar to those of the early 928, fog lights were incorporated in the front apron, an improved deflector was installed in the sunroof, seals were improved on the Targa and Carrera badges fixed to the engine cover. The Turbo's improved heating system was incorporated. American versions also received an upshift indicator on the facia.

Year	Body	Type	Chassis number	Engine type	6-cylinder bore x stroke	C.R.	Power bhp/rpm	Torque lb/ft
1983/84	Coupe	911 Carrera	WPO22291ZES100001- WPO22291ZES104033	930/20	95×74.4 (3,164cc)	10.3:1	231 @ 5,900	209 @ 4,800
	Targa	911 Carrera	WPO22291ZES140001- WPO22291ZES141469	930/20	95×74.4	10.3:1	231 @ 5,900	209 @ 4,800
	Cabrio	911 Carrera	WPO22291ZES150001- WPO22291ZES151835	930/20	95×74.4	10.3:1	231 @ 5,900	209 @ 4,800
	Coupe	911 Carr-US	WPOABO91ES120001- WPOABO91ES122282	930/21	95×74.4	9.5:1	202 @ 5,900	185 @ 4,800
	Targa	911 Carr-US	WPOEBO91ES160001- WPOEBO91ES162260	930/21	95×74.4	9.5:1	202 @ 5,900	185 @ 4,800
	Cabrio	911 Carr-US	WPOEBO91ES170001- WPOEBO91ES171191	930/21	95×74.4	9.5:1	202 @ 5,900	185 @ 4,800
	Coupe	911 Carr-Japan	WPO22291ZES109501- WPO22291ZES109717	930/21	95×74.4	9.5:1	202 @ 5,900	185 @ 4,800
	Targa	911 Carr-Japan	WPO22291ZES149501- WPO22291ZES149564	930/21	95×74.4	9.5:1	202 @ 5,900	185 @ 4,800
	Cabrio	911 Carr-Japan	WPO22291ZES159501- WPO22291ZES159577	930/21	95×74.4	9.5:1	202 @ 5,900	185 @ 4,800
	Coupe	930	WPO22293ZES000001- WPO11193ZES000804	930/66	97×74.4 (3,299cc)	7.0:1	300 @ 5,500	318 @ 4,000
	Coupe	930-Canada	WPOJAO93ES05001- WPOJAO93ES050077	930/66	97×74.4	7.0:1	300 @ 5,500	318 @ 4,000

F Series. The 1985 model year saw detailed improvements only. The front seats were made to a new specification with the backrest height increased by 40mm. All models had electrical adjustment for seat height and rake (not reach, however) and the Carrera could be ordered with electrically heated seats, standard on the Turbo. Central locking, standard on the Turbo, was optional for the Carrera. The Carrera's gear lever was reduced in length, a four-spoke steering wheel adopted, and the radio aerial was incorporated as an element in the windscreen, a safety Sekuriflex glass screen being optional. Electrically heated windscreen washer nozzles also became standard.

The Turbo model received a revised brake booster to lower pedal pressures and the front/rear anti-roll bars were increased in diameter by 2mm, to 22mm at the front and 20mm at the rear.

Year	Body	Type	Chassis number	Engine type	6-cylinder bore x stroke	C.R.	Power bhp/rpm	Torque lb/ft
1984/85	Coupe	911 Carrera	WPO22291ZFS100001-	930/20	95×74.4	10.3:1	231 @ 5,900	209 @ 4,800
	Targa	911 Carrera	WPO22291ZFS140001-	930/20	95×74.4	10.3:1	231 @ 5,900	209 @ 4,800
	Cabrio	911 Carrera	WPO22291ZFS150001-	930/20	95×74.4	10.3:1	231 @ 5,900	209 @ 4,800
	Coupe	911 Carr-US	WPOABO91FS120001-	930/21	95×74.4	9.5:1	202 @ 5,900	185 @ 4,800
	Targa	911 Carr-US	WPOEBO91FS160001-	930/21	95×74.4	9.5:1	202 @ 5,900	185 @ 4,800
	Cabrio	911 Carr-US	WPOEBO91FS170001-	930/21	95×74.4	9.5:1	202 @ 5,900	185 @ 4,800
	Coupe	911 Carr-Japan	WPO22291ZFS109501-	930/21	95×74.4	9.5:1	202 @ 5,900	185 @ 4,800
	Targa	911 Carr-Japan	WPO22291ZFS149501-	930/21	95×74.4	9.5:1	202 @ 5,900	185 @ 4,800
	Cabrio	911 Carr-Japan	WPO22291ZFS159501-	930/21	95×74.4	9.5:1	202 @ 5,900	185 @ 4,800
	Coupe	930	WPO22293ZFS000001-	930/66	97×74.4 (3,299cc)	7.0:1	300 @ 5,500	318 @ 4,000
	Coupe	930-Canada	WPOJAO93FS050001-	930/66	97×74.4	7.0:1	300 @ 5,500	318 @ 4,000

*Our thanks are due to Juergen Barth and Lothar Boschen for their work in compiling the data on chassis numbers, with acknowledgement to *Das Grosse Buch der Porsche-typen,* and the publishers Motorbuch-Verlag, Stuttgart.

Typical Porsche 911 and Turbo performance figures

The following data is compiled from leading motoring journals, usually *Motor* or *Autocar*, using sophisticated equipment to measure performance. Results tend to be a little inconsistent and are, generally, more favourable than the factory's claimed performance figures. Fuel consumptions, however, tend to reflect high-speed testing and are at the top end of a normal touring range.

Year	Model	Acceleration		Maximum speed	Overall mpg (Imp)
		0-60 mph	0-100 mph		
1965	911 2.0	8.7	24.1	130	21.1
	912	11.9	38.5	119	23.6
1966	911S 2.0	7.3	19.2	137	17.6
1968	911L 2.0 Sportomatic	9.8	23.7	127	17.6
1969	911T 2.2	8.1	23.7	129	18.9
	911E 2.2	7.6	20.8	137	18.5
	911S 2.2	6.5	18.1	140	16.8
1971	911T 2.4	8.9	22.5	131	18.8
	911E 2.4	7.5	19.5	137	18.0
	911S 2.4	6.2	17.1	145	15.3
1973	911 Carrera 2.7 RST	5.5	14.9	150	16.7
1975	911 2.7	7.2	19.4	136	18.4
	911S 2.7	6.5	18.3	140	19.8
	Carrera 3	5.7	15.5	145	18.2
	Turbo 3.0	6.1	14.5	153	18.5
1977	911SC 3.0	6.5	17.9	141	17.9
1978	Turbo 3.3	5.3	12.3	160	15.9
1980	911SC 3.0	5.7	15.8	148	20.4
1983	911 3.2 Carrera	5.3	13.6	152	21.1
	Turbo 3.3	5.1	12.2	162	16.4
1986	959 4-wd (factory figs)	4.8	n/a	186	n/a

Competition cars, 1965-1985
911, 934, 935 and 959

Year	Type	Chassis number	Engine type	Capacity mm/cc	bhp DIN	Torque lb/ft	Weight Kg
1965	911-2.0 'Monte'	303075 303076 303077	901/02	80×66 1,991	160 @ 6,600	134 @ 5,200	1,030
1967	911-2.0 'Rally'	306655S 306656S 306657S	901/30	80×66 1,991	170 @ 7,300	134 @ 5,200	1,030
	911R-2.0	307670 307671 305876 118990001R	901/22	80×66 1,991	210 @ 8,000	152 @ 6,000	800
1970	911S-2.2 'Rally'	9110300001 9110300002 9110300003 9110300949 9110300950	911/02	84×66 2,195	180 @ 6,500	147 @ 5,200	960
	911S-2.3	911030001 911030002 911030003	911/20	85×66 2,247	240 @ 7,800	166 @ 6,300	840
	911S-2.4	911030949	911/21	85×70.4 2,395	260 @ 8,000	181 @ 6,500	790
1971	911S-2.2	9111300637 9111300683	911/02	84×66 2,195	180 @ 6,500	147 @ 5,200	980
	'Safari'	911300561 911300589 911300612	911/02	84×66 2,195	180 @ 6,500	147 @ 5,200	980
1972	911S-2.5	9112300041 to 047	911/73 & 911/70	89×66 2,466 & 86.7×70.4 2,492	270 @ 8,000	192 @ 6,300	960
1973	911 Carrera 2.7 Safari	9113600285 9113600288	911/83	90×70.4 2,687	210 @ 6,300	188 @ 5,100	980
	Carrera	9113600386 to 01549 (49 made)	911/72	92×70.4 2,806	300 @ 8,000	217 @ 6,500	900
	Carrera RSR 'proto'	911360019-R1 0020-R2 0307-R3 0328-R4 0576-R5 0588-R6 0686-R7 0974-R8	911/72 & 911/74 & 911/75	92×70.4 2,806 / 95×70.4 2,993 / 95×70.4 2,993	300 @ 8,000 / 315 @ 8,000 / 330 @ 8,000	217 @ 6,500 / 231 @ 6,500 / 231 @ 6,500	850
1974	Carrera RS 3.0	9114609001 to 9109	911/77	95×70.4 2,993	230 @ 6,200	202 @ 5,000	920
	Carrera RSR 3.0	–	911/75	95×70.4 2,993	330 @ 8,000	231 @ 6,500	900
	Carrera 'Proto' t/c	9113600576-R5 9114609016-R9	911/76	83×66 2,142	450 @ 8,000	333 @ 5,500	750
		9114609101-R12 9114609102-R13	911/78	83×66 2,142	500 @ 7,600	405 @ 5,400	820
1976	934 Turbo Gp 4	9306700151 to 0180 9306700540	930/75	95×70.4 2,993	485 @ 7,000	434 @ 5,400	1,120
	935 Turbo Gp 5	930570002-R15 935.001 935.002	930/72	92×70.4 2,806	590 @ 7,900	434 @ 5,400	970
1977	934 Turbo US	9307700951 to 00960	930/73	95×70.4 2,993	540 @ 7,000	434 @ 5,400	1,120
	935 Turbo	9307700901 to 913	930/72	92.8×70.4 2,857	590 @ 7,900	434 @ 5,400	970
	935-77	935.77003 77004 77005	930/78	92×70.4 2,857	630 @ 8,000	434 @ 5,400	970
	935-77 'Baby'	935.02001	911/79	71×60 1,425	370 @ 8,000	n/a	730
1978	911SC 3.0 'Safari'	9118300789 9118301416	911/77	95×70.4 2,994	250 @ 6,800	220 @ 5,500	1,300

Year	Type	Chassis number	Engine type	Capacity mm/cc	bhp DIN	Torque lb/ft	Weight Kg
		9118301474 9118301476					
	935-78	9308900011	930/72	92.8×70.4 2,857	600 @ 8,000	434 @ 5,400	970
		9308900033	930/78	95×70.4 2,994	675 @ 8,000	528 @ 5,600	1,025
		Engines supplied:					
			930/79	97×70.4 3,124	680 @ 8,000	520 @ 5,600	
			930/80	95×74.4 3,160	720 @ 8,000	542 @ 5,500	
	935-78 'Moby Dick'	935.006 935.007	935/3.2	95.7×74.4 3,211	750 @ 8,200	615 @ 6,500	1,025

Year	Type	Chassis number	Engine type	Capacity mm/cc	bhp DIN	Torque lb/ft	Weight Kg
1979	935-79	93500016 93500017 93500022 to 00028	930/80	95×74.4 3,160	720 @ 8,000	542 @ 5,500	1,025
1981	911SC 3.0 Rally	WPO22291ZCS100338	911/81R	95×70.4 2,993	230 @ 7,800	200 @ 5,600	1,070
1983	911 4-wd Paris-Dakar	WPO22291ZES100020 100021 100022	953/84	95×74.4 3,160	225 @ 6,000	203 @ 4,700	1,215
1984	959 Paris-Dakar	WPO22293ZFS010001 010014 010015	953/85	95×74.4 3,160	230 @ 6,000	206 @ 5,000	1,185

Porsche Clubs

Listed below are the national Porsche Clubs around the world, but there are many more. There is a Porsche Club in virtually every major town and city in Germany, several in Switzerland and Austria and regional clubs throughout America. Porsche importers in each country will have a list of recognized clubs, or details may be obtained from Frau Naedele, Porsche Clubs Co-ordinator at Dr Ing hc F Porsche AG, Porschestrasse 15-19, D-7140, Ludwigsburg, Germany.

Porsche Club of America
Sec: Sandi Misura
1753 Las Gallina
San Rafael
California 94903
USA

Porsche Club Argentina
Sec: David Santana
Avenida Santa Fe 950
1640 Acussuso
Buenos Aires
Argentina

Porsche Club Deutschland
Sec: Manfred Pfeiffer
Podbielskiallee 25-27
D-1000 Berlin 33
W. Germany

Porsche Club Great Britain
Sec: Roy Gillham
64 Raisins Hill
Pinner
Middlesex

Porsche Club of Western Australia
Sec: Rob Jones
PO Box 447
South Perth
Western Australia 6151

Porsche Club of NSW
Sec: John Clark
PO Box 183
Lindfield NSW 2070
Sydney, Australia

Porsche Club Hongkong
No 1 Yip Fat Street
PO Box 24539
Aberdeen Post Office
Wong Chuk Hang
Aberdeen, Hong Kong

Porsche Club Italia
Sec: Gabriella Bigontina
Via Carlo Osma 2
I-20151 Milano
Italy

Austria: Porsche Club Wien
Sec: Ing Udo Poeschmann
Mariahilfer Str 19-21
A-1060 Vienna

Porsche Club Belgique
50 Rue du Mail
B-1050
Brussels

Porsche Club of Japan
Sec: H. Sumitani
c/o Mitsuwa Motors Co Ltd
No 18-6 Roppongi 3-Chome
Minato-Ku
Tokyo 106
Japan

Porsche Club Luxembourg
Sec: J. Frast
c/o Novotel
E42-route d'Echternach
L-1453 Luxembourg-Dommeldang

Porsche Club of Brazil
Sec: Claudio Tozzi
Rua Nigeria 121
BR-04538 Sao Paulo

Porsche Club Denmark
Sec: Flemming L. Nielsen
Ved Jaegerdiget 9A
DK-2670 Greve Strand

Nederlandse Porsche Club
Van Alkemadelaan 878
Den Haag
Netherlands

Porsche Club Holland
Sec: P. Polle
Wim Sonneveldlaan 227
NL-3584 ZS Utrecht
Netherlands

Porsche Club Suomi-Finland
Sec: Klaus Kingelin
Sipilan Kartano
SF-12380 Lappakoski
Finland

Porsche Club de France
Sec: Marc Tripels
c/o Sonauto SA
1 Avenue du Fief
BP 479
F-95005 Cergy Pontoise Cedex
France

Porsche Club of New Zealand
Sec: J. Robertson
204 Beach Road
Campbells Bay
Auckland
New Zealand

Porsche Club Norway
Sec: Johannes Bidesbøl
Postboks 32
Lysejordet
N-Oslo 7
Norway

Porsche Club Sweden
Sec: Stina Liljeberg
Postbox 340 25
S-10026 Stockholm
Sweden

Porsche Club Spain
Sec: Inmaculada Sanz
Paseo de la Castellana 240
Madrid 16
Spain

Porsche Club of South Africa
Sec: Angela Hausler
PO Box 9834
Johannesburg 2000
South Africa

Porsche Club Romand
Sec: Philippe Collet
Chateau 13
CH-1806 St Legier
Switzerland

Porsche Club Zurich
Sec: Roland Studer
c/o Oscar Senn-Bucher
Boldistrasse 76
CH-5414 Rieden-Bussbaumen
Switzerland